THE MOURNING LIGHT

REFLECTIONS ON LOVE AND LOSS

RACHEL DESROCHERS

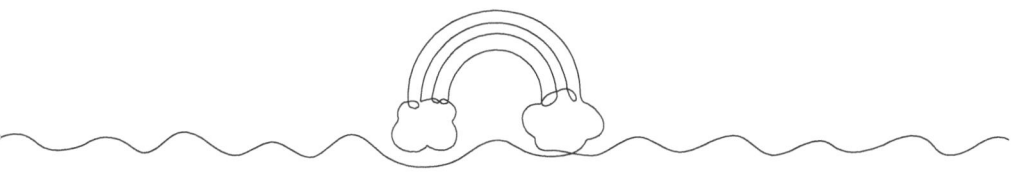

The Mourning Light: Reflections on Love & Loss
Copyright © 2025 by Rachel DesRochers
Published by VITALITY buzz, bliss + books LLC
vitalitybuzz.org

VITALITY
buzz, bliss + books

ISBN: 978-1-954688-29-2

To my mom, thank you for teaching me to always love bigger. I am so proud that I am your daughter. Thank you for being my muse & reminding me anything is possible. I love you & miss you so much!

To my kids, Camden, Rosalee & Ellis, it's the greatest honor of my life being your mom. These words, this work, every moment so I can be my best self for you all. My greatest loves & biggest reason for wanting to dream bigger, thank you! I love you all so much!

To my incredible family, dad, Kare, sister, brother, aunts & uncles, the Greats too!

To my sisters, who have literally picked me up time & time again, no questions asked.

To Stephanie for time with these words, with me, her tenderness & care as I birthed this book.

To the VITALITY team for making publishing a book possible.

To the **fenbury** team for the art & cover, holding so much space for this project!

To Ali for triple checking my recipes.

To my companies & team members, thank you for working alongside me, I couldn't do it without you.

To my community, yes you, thank you. You make me want to show up every single day and be present with you. It's such a privilege.

in gratitude

to the VATRONS
who breathed life into this book
by pre-ordering their copy

Rebeca Arbona, Carol Arrom, Marla Barone, Gretchen Bayer, Stephanie Beck Borden, Amy Benetti, Desiré Bennett, Abby Blair, Burns Blaxall, Lauren Boehm, Lauren Boehmker, Holly Brians Ragusa, Emily Brown, Pam Cho, Sara Clifton, Kerry Conley, Alison Crowdus, Gillian Cruce, Kimberly Darpel, Karen Deime, Julie Doepke, Jennifer Dreyer, Lisa Dugan-Manor, Amie Duncan, Whitney Ellison, LaTrisha Fail, Denise Fenik, Elisabeth Galperin, Heather Gerker, Camden Grubbs, Lorrie Hayes, Tara Heilman, Mary Huss, Megan Jackson, Rivanna Jihan, Megan Jones, Sarah Jordan, Alexandra Kell, Jesse Kelly, Emily Kimball, April Kline, Claire Krawsczyn, Stephanie Kruthaupt, Ann Lafferty, Brianna Ledsome, Cathy Lindemann, Tara Litmer, Teah Longland, Deborah Malave, Catherine Manabat, Melissa Marie, Stacey McIntyr, Amy Mersch, Meghan Metzger, Sarah Mohr, Kelley Moore, Nickol Mora, Lauren Murphy, Julie Navarre, Sue Newman, Jackie O'Connell, Brittany Obryan, Julie Payne, Tian Philson, Krista Powers, Heather Richard, Kristel Rubio, Shannon Sherrard, Brian Shircliff, Rakhi Srivastava, Aly Stacy, Christina Stalbaum, Martha Tepe, Jenny Watts, Alicia Wilhelmy, Theresa Wilmot, Kelly Wittry, Kyla Woods, Lauren Worley, Cynthia Wright Sellers, Kate Zink

CONTENTS

This is part memoir, part memories, part workbook.

This is my heart, exploding onto pages.

It's impactful moments and how they've transformed me.

These words are the way that I remember it all
the best that I can.

My earliest and most defining memories involve my mom and
the way she fed people. I find comfort in the kitchen. For me
food is the ultimate connector for community building and it is
why my life is so heavily focused on that space. I'm a foodie.
The recipes in this book are my favorites. I use them daily or
weekly. I grew up watching my mom, Mary, make them, and I
believe they're a great way to close out each chapter—feed
your heart, feed your belly.

one

The Forgetting

My earliest memories of my mom are when I would sit on the dryer while she did laundry and she would make me spell word after word after word. We lived in a four family building where some of our pastimes were putting glue on our hands to dry then peel off (ok right, total party animals) and snapping green beans one by one. "Peel that string out Rachel....Oops, you are snapping too much off, Rachel." Mom moved around the kitchen with ease and grace. There were always recipes in piles and stacks around the kitchen and hundreds of books and binders, but never once did she follow a single recipe. I loved learning how comfort, love, and a few seasonings make the dish. My mom fed me in so many incredible ways.

I remember when I first noticed the forgetting. See, my mom and I, we were close—like, talk four times a day, what are you doing this weekend, hey let's take a vacation together, close. I've always been smitten with my parents. They are fun to be around, and even as a teen, I spent more time hanging with them on the weekends than doing cool teen things. That's how close we were (or maybe I was just that cool, haha).

I have memories of Mom calling to say, "Hey, Rach, let's go to lunch."

Sometimes, I would reply with, "Oh, Mom, I'm sorry, I can't today. I have a full day of work."

"Oh, fine," she would say, and hastily hang up.

Then, her return call within 30 minutes, "Hey sis, what are you doing today? Want to hang?"

"Oh, hey Mom. How's it going?" In my mind, I'm thinking, WTF is wrong Mary? I just told you I am working and pretty slammed today, so I really need to get back to it.

How do I gently tell her I can't go again? And again. And again. Those calls were how it all started for me; recognizing the slow drift she was beginning.

I called Dad after a few months of this consistent behavior asking, "Hey, do you recognize this? What do we do?" He was watching his best friend, his partner, drift away and not accepting it.

I remember taking her to the neurologist. The test—oh, the test. They gave her a series of problems to solve and well, to say she failed would be an understatement. But also Mary was in there fully and vibrantly.

I remember her childlike giggle as she filled in the face of a clock, ever so gently looking around the room for an example to follow. She would beat this damn thing if she pleased. And boy did she try, but numbers and lines were misplaced, 1 2 3 6 9, not where they were supposed to be. She pretty much told the doc to shove it, that she was fine, there "ain't nothing wrong'" and that their tests suck.

My heart sank because I knew with that defaced clock that her drift away from us was not something small or temporary, the countdown officially started and her time with us wouldn't last near as long as I had hoped. At the age of 59 my mom was diagnosed with early onset Alzheimer's. The average life expectancy is four to five years if you're lucky. It was one of the most brutiful (beautiful + brutal) experiences I have witnessed.

This book is about losing my mom, but it's also about how grief expanded to every crevice in my being and shined light on how to live each day finding healing and joy. It is about how grief and gratitude can bring the fullness of this world to our fingertips, and how dealing with our own suffering is the key to unlocking freedom, joy, and the fullness we deserve.

I have given gratitude public praise for a long time. Each word in this book is filled with gratitude. When I speak to groups I always teach the practice. It is me, I am it. And in healing, in facing death in the eyes, my own and hers, I realize right next to grief is gratitude. Gratitude changed my life but grief has expanded me, showing me that we have the opportunity to live in joy and hope every day instead of fear and anxiety. I am grateful for the awakening that they both brought forward in my life.

That diagnosis changed everything. It confirmed my fears. It brought death to my lips. It showed both how fast time goes and how it feels as if it never moves. It humanized me. It also taught me how a woman from Honeybee, Kentucky pushed past everything she was told—you can't, you won't, not you— and built the life of her dreams. I experienced how a big heart and an open home brought riches that money could never buy. I also learned this lesson that will be consistently woven throughout this story:

LIFE IS LOVE.

After we wept, after we accepted—or didn't accept—this diagnosis, after we allowed ourselves to know that these moments would be our last, I knew I could never take for granted any moment with her. How could I give her the best last years, the best death? What a blessing that we KNEW— as hard as those last years may have been, we had them. I did not take that time for granted. Those long days or hard moments were an invitation for me to accept the duality of living and dying at the same time.

We all are here - in our own living and our own dying. But how do we move forward from a moment knowing that we are HERE and ALIVE? Let's LIVE. We can choose to be small, play small, live small because it's easier than digging and doing the more challenging work to push through our stories and build the life of our dreams. It is never too late to choose to be fully present in wonder and awe, in grief and gratitude for being alive right now. What an incredible gift, for each of us.

I encourage you to take a deep breath, feel your heart, let your shoulders drop—yes, right now, in the middle of chapter one. Breathe. Feel your pulse. Feel the heat coming out of your mouth as you exhale. Feel your nostrils expand and fill with air as you inhale. Settle in. You are here.

That is an incredible gift. Let us move from this moment not taking that for granted, determined to understand how we stay ecstatic in living through the trials and tribulations that are life. That is living. Permission granted.

Today is the first day of the rest of your life.

And that's what I did:

Family vacations

Weekends drinking margaritas (Mom's favorite besides a glass—or bottle—of pinot noir and a close second of one of our favorite local breweries Madtree's Lift)

Shopping and thrifting

Family dinners

Birthday celebrations and photos, videos and being present.

She was ALIVE, and I didn't want to miss one moment.

Dad and I laugh about it now. Those vacations were breaks for us both in many ways during that season. He would hang with my littles, and I would take Mom out for adventures, each watching the other's "kids" and getting away from our normal day to day lives. I am glad my children witnessed me tending to her, the mothering of the mother. We want to protect our kids from death, but I wanted to make sure my kids knew their grandmother, even a dying one.

My mom never accepted her diagnosis. She never accepted that she was sick or that something was wrong. She knew her time was being cut short, and as hard as it was for us when she fought the fact that something was wrong, I can't imagine how trapped this woman who was so full of life felt. How do we accept it when they won't? How do we make this reality part of our normal everyday life? How do we love them so deeply and for a moment put our own wants and worries aside (come on Mom, it would just be easier for US if you did this, accept it lady, you're sick) and let them get through this the way that they need to. For her, she needed to stay strong, like nothing was wrong. She needed to find joy and activity around every corner.

Telling a grown woman she can't drive isn't easy. My dad, the good man that he is, never really told my mom no in their 43 years of marriage. He truly made any of her asks come true. Nothing was too big or too small. She told me for two years, post diagnosis, that he was buying her a new car. That was always a fun one to navigate. "Oh ya Mom, you are going to look so great in a new car." That was until we lost her—literally. She got lost in her car. My dad jokes about calling to tell me he lost her and how that may have been one of the scariest moments of his life. It was a miracle she found her way back home. We had driven around for an hour or more looking for her. We even called the auto shop where she was dropping her car off but they hadn't seen her. Her angels brought her home, though she wouldn't admit it. She was scared, you could see it in her eyes, like a scolded child who knew she did something wrong even if she wasn't quite sure what it was. And though she fought it, she stopped driving after that. Still, she believed Dad was going to buy her a new car, so she waited for that day to come so she could drive again. Oh Mary.

I accepted her diagnosis the best way I knew how, she did the same. It took her heart attack in March 2020 for my Dad to finally accept it. We all have to find our way on our own time, worrying less about how we want things to be and instead accepting them for what is and what's needed. I had plenty of things that got me through this but the tool I used every day was my gratitude practice.

Every day, I spent time reflecting on the good we still got to experience with her. Every day, I spent time thinking about the greatness that was my mother. Every day I spent time noticing my cup overflowing even when it was so hard and I couldn't face one more moment. Every day, I spent time reflecting on moments and memories.

Gratitude made space for my grief and held me closely, reminding me of my own strength, the lessons for living she passed on to all of us, and how truly even this experience would produce miracles I wasn't expecting...Gratitude + Grief.

No longer alone in practice. No longer alone in my heart.

Gratitude helped me not be afraid of grief. Dying is part of life. Grief is part of life. How do I shine light on these words, experiences, and heaviness that are so unfamiliar? How do I make sure I am not swallowed up by grief and stop doing the very thing she taught me to do—live and celebrate being HERE. At the same time, there were absolutely moments when grief swallowed me whole and I didn't know how to mother or wife or work. It was a both/and experience so the lesson was to not get stuck, to try to hold it as lightly as possible.

Let's be honest, in those early days after her diagnosis, we had good times. Alzheimer's folks are sweet and funny. Asking Ellis to read her poems. Her "art clusters" as I would call them, where she would gather items from all over the house and make displays with them. I have a ton of photos of cowboy boots, tissues, and stuffed animals all piled together. Her art, her offering. She would say random things and wear crazy outfits. Trying to keep up with her out in public was a challenge because Lordy she may not have been there mentally but her body and spirits never slowed down. She was a tiny gal, but she was strong as an ox. No one would ever challenge her to an arm wrestling match because she would school you. So much of her remained for so long, and what a miracle that was. Having her heart but not her mind. At least we had something.

I am grateful for my mom, for this experience, for her death, for the lessons that came with it and how all of these parts expanded me. I am grateful I wasn't afraid of her dying or of letting grief settle in my body. I am grateful for how this experience has impacted my life and also allowed me to share these lessons with others. I am grateful for flashbacks of snapping green beans, forcing my kids to do the same and wondering if she had to force me, too. I am grateful for that time I took, the things that fell to the side so that I could be with her. I am grateful for the love her and my dad shared, and that they showed me every day how to love through hard things. I am grateful to be in her home, her house on the hill that is now mine, and feel her in every corner. I am grateful that she instilled in me this wonder and awe. I am grateful she loved so damn big, no matter who you were or where you came from. My mom would always make room and include you. No one was too good or not good enough. That is big love.

I wrote and shared this on social media March 10, 2020 in a glimpse of that all consuming grief.

Grief is a funny thing. It's a process I am familiar with as I started grieving the loss of my mother three years ago with her early onset Alzheimer's diagnosis.

This grief right now is for us to keep living in light.

You want to honor the work and love of Mary - then be kind to one another. Buy the shoes you love, heck she wouldn't even care if they fit, she'd say buy them. Adorn yourself in your finest jewels of all time. Have the wine. Go for walks. Laugh and if you are thinking of someone, call them. These are just a few of the lessons that my mama taught me.

In March of 2020, our entire world shifted. By miracles and miracles alone, she came back to us for a short while. Those stories will unfold in these pages. I was learning to walk with living and grieving.

So let's go back a bit.

I am the middle child. My sister is seven years older than me. If you met her she would tell you I ruined her seventh birthday because on her seventh birthday, April 7, my mom went into labor with me, and I was born on April 8. Seven years and one day apart from one another. I still remind her, "At least you got seven years solo. Lucky."

My brother is eight years younger than me. He was the first boy born in our family in over twenty seven years and that meant something. He was also my bestie, but I think I pretended I was his mom more than anything. I made sure he didn't go without, even when he wasn't asking for a darn thing.

I was smack dab in the middle of them. I can relate to most things said about the middle child. With the years between us, we each received special, individual attention in our early years. We all missed parts of each other's lives because when my little brother was going through high school, I was already a mom, and my sister had already been out on her own for years. I think Mom had us so far apart because she came from a family of fourteen kids. She knew the pressure and burden of back to back babies, of kids becoming parents. She didn't speak much about it but I think she probably helped take care of so many siblings, as most big families do, that she enjoyed having one at a time to really tend to. I respect that.

And I love being in the middle.

In grade school, I was the dorky gal with matching tracksuits. As I was about to enter 6th grade, we moved so I started at a new school. What a terrible time to do that as a full bodied kid; that year shaped me in ways that I still share with people. I was eleven or twelve years old. This lesson, this experience changed me. I love sharing this story because we all need to hear these words whether at seven or eleven or thirty-two or sixty-three. I recognized it then as a life changing moment, I honor it now as a life changing experience.

I remember coming home from school and sobbing, "Why don't they like me? Why do they make fun of me? Why am I not good enough for them?"

My dad looked at me, as any dad would—the eyes that say I'm sorry and here's a life lesson.

He said, "They don't love themselves, Rachel."

Me: ....

Him, "Love yourself. You are enough. You are beautiful. Love yourself for who you are. They don't get it. They are enough, too, but no one is telling them that or they wouldn't be mean."

Me: ....

Oh, I am enough. I am beautiful. I love myself for me.

By the grace of God, that lesson touched my soul, I heard him. I heard the words, but not only did I hear them, I understood them.

Be kind. Be love.

I was eleven. So when people ask me, how did you get like this, how do you understand this stuff, my only response is that it's the way I've always been. I can't understand it, I don't question it, but I can have immense gratitude for it.

The next lesson, Dad said to be grateful for the experience and the learning.

BE GRATEFUL FOR WHO YOU ARE.

And then my life became that. A life of gratitude at age eleven.

Don't get me wrong, I was still a kid, a smart ass at that. Strong, not defiant for breaking rules, but willing to ask questions and push against the "that's the way that it is" mentality.

I got in trouble in high school for passing gratitude journals through class.

I was scolded in my high school religious ed class for playing Ani DiFranco's song about abortion.

I became pregnant during my senior year in high school. At an all girl Catholic high school.

I am a college dropout.

I left a 20-year marriage that was entangled with addiction and found my voice again.

And so much more.

Gratitude and all, I still made decisions I had to learn from. As a matter of fact, I still do. Though I've learned to listen better.

I don't have any regrets. These experiences shaped me, they've allowed me to fall and get back up. I am here because I walked through them. Even in hardship, gratitude never left my mind. There is a divinity when we get out of the way, when we accept the pain and the lessons that come with our decisions. Of course, when I am in the middle of the pain, the lesson, it can be hard to navigate. Gratitude helps pull me out of the trench of despair to see the light. I am proud of my scars and stretch marks and soul.

Before we move forward I want to define gratitude, show you how I practice it and how I've learned to understand the fullness of the word. I've studied it. It's my life's mission and purpose. So as this book will give many examples of how gratitude has shown up in my life, it's also an invitation for you to start a practice today that will change your life. Gratitude will continue building fullness and abundance in your life like no other tool can.

I've been practicing gratitude in some way or another for over three decades so I always joke that gratitude is my strongest muscle.

Gratitude is:

1. The greatest spiritual tool you will ever use.
2. Ever expanding.
3. Free & inclusive of who you are, where you are in your life journey, financial status, gender, race - IT IS FOR ALL.
4. Complete in the sense that no matter what you are going through or experiencing, gratitude doesn't ignore or take away that experience. Grief and sorrow can sit with joy and peace.

Gratitude works because it doesn't diminish your experience. Gratitude shines the tiniest little light. The practice allows the light to be present while acknowledging the grief, the pain, the sadness, the confusion, anger, the frustration.

It says: Be afraid and feel love.

It's ok to feel the pain and celebrate the occasion. Process the grief and look at the joyous abundance.

There is no lack here. If you are struggling with an abundance mindset, this is the first piece to freedom.

Gratitude comes to sit gently in your lap. It's a breath. It reassures us that it's ok to be sad and find joy. It's the "and" that is so powerful.

It is the yin and yang.

Gratitude got me through some of the poorest days of my entrepreneur journey. How are we going to feed the kids and buy shoes and pay the bills? Marinating in fear and worry didn't change what was happening, so I turned to gratitude: I am grateful for our home, warm water, handmade blankets, and potlucks. I created a Saturday Supper Club during those days when we were most broke—we could not eat more beans & rice. Guess what? Our community showed up and fed us. We fed each other.

I started my first company, Grateful Grahams, with $1000. If I was going to put this practice into action, creating my dreams, spreading a message I believed in, I knew I had to just start. So I took what experience I had in marketing and in food, creating a company around it. Starting Grateful Grahams was the hardest and most rewarding thing I have ever done. Even though I closed the company at the end of 2023 I wouldn't be here without what that company gave to me - a platform, a voice and a deeper belief that I'd change the world through the message of gratitude.

I risked a lot starting companies without financial backing. I am a worker, a hard worker. The workload never frightened me, even thinking back to how hard those early days were. I am proud I never gave up. I credit a lot of that back to this practice of gratitude. No matter how dark it got, this practice reminded me of what I had—healthy kids, friends who love me, and a community that cares.

That is gratitude in action.

Gratitude doesn't diminish or whitewash the hard parts. That, to me, is the key.

Our mind doesn't believe the idea that writing or texting 3-5 things a day we are grateful for can actually change our life. However, I am proof it can. It's in the simplicity that the true power lies.

It's in the simplicity that the true healing lies.

Gratitude honors you—right here, with what you have and where you are. It says, I see you AND...

I think that is so important here. That's the magic. It allows ALL of you to be present. Your whole being. It acknowledges the suffering and allows the jubilation to join. It's the AND, it's the breath, it's everything.

Stop questioning it and start practicing today.

So, I guess now that it's defined, how do we use it? It's simple. I encourage us all to start here. This next page is blank for you to start your practice with today's list.

Now, before you begin: 1. It really is this simple. 2. Type it, write it, text it. It doesn't matter—just DO IT. That is what matters. If you are the person that needs a special pen and notebook— order it right now. Or perhaps use my **Shift to Light: 90 Days to Grateful** gratitude journal.

If you are a notes app person, pull a new one up on your phone or tablet and label it Gratitude List.

If you have a group of friends that could support this journey, start a text chain that is only for 3-5 gratitudes a day.

I encourage you to try and name twelve things you are grateful for. If you are in a flow, keep pouring them out. There are never too many. Try for at least three things, minimum.

I am always grateful for morning tea. I am always grateful for my bed. I am always grateful for clean drinking water.

It's never about the outside world. Turn inward, be present with your heart. Take a deep breath, slowly exhale, and begin.

I am grateful for:

1.

2.

3.

4.

5.

6.

7.

8.

9.

10.

11.

12.

13.

14.

15.

16.

17.

18.

19.

20.

On 6/26/22 I wrote:

I am writing this faster than my fingers can keep up with here are some things I am grateful for:

Office space at our home.

Hanging at the pool with the family.

Home cooked meals of comfort.

Buying sis a bathing suit.

Dog sitting Emily while Dad is out of town.

A phone that can play music, right at my fingertips.

Having space for these words to come out.

My house Birkenstocks and how they are worn so perfectly.

The blessing of air conditioning.

Being in my mother's house and how she is so present here for me still.

This breath, the practice of being here.

Morning pages and how in just one month it's opened my heart so much.

Black Eyed Peas

1 lb black eye peas, dried
2 cups carrot, diced
2 cups celery, diced
4 cups yellow onion, diced
4 cloves garlic, minced
2 bay leaves
salt & pepper
8 -10 cups of broth (i love the vegan chik'n bouillon)

Instructions:

Soak your beans. Get a big bowl, dump your beans in & cover with water. I normally run my hands through them, moving them around. As Mary would say - checking for rocks. I am not sure I have ever found a rock, but golly I check for them every time. Dump that water & recover. Let them sit out overnight. There are ways to quickly do this but I don't know nor have I ever attempted to do that. This is how my mama made these and well, this is how I make them.

The next day when you are ready to start cooking, rinse the beans really well. I usually dump them in my strainer and rinse well.

Now, I normally omit the oil here but if you want add 1-2 tbs olive oil in your pan. If you're skipping it like me I just add a couple tablespoons of water.

Salt - A good pinch of salt here when I say salt it. Salt is your friend.

Add water to your pot. Add your onion, salt your onion, stir it around good and let it cook til near translucent. Add your carrot, celery & garlic. Salt it again. Stir it all together & let it cook 5-7 minutes while those veggies get happy.

Add your black eyed peas. Stir it all together & well, add another pinch of salt.

Add your broth of choice and bay leaves. Cover with about an inch or two OVER the beans & veggies. Bring to a boil & then turn down to simmer.

Stir every hour or so. You may need to add more water (keep your beans covered)

I usually let it cook for about 2 hours or my beans are soft. Taste it. Does it need more salt? Add another good pinch. Eat & enjoy. It will be even better tomorrow. Beans are just great like that.

two

The Dying

Death. It is a beautiful, holy thing. Going back to this space where there are no machines, just us and our heartbeats and our love, that death. A death where the last breath is taken. My grandfather's death is holy. He is a good man. Not just because he's my grandpa, but because he led with love. Because he never met a stranger. Because when he was a sharpshooter and was being sent out to Wounded Knee, he said no way will I go out there and kill the innocent. Because he loved his family. Because he had strong hands and even stronger stories. Because he is my father's father. Because his blood is mine. Because he would give you the shirt off his back if he knew it would bring you comfort. Because he would tell you - YES get two scoops and go pick out a treat for later. Because he is a divine being who will forever watch over us all.

Those are words I wrote in February 2018, reading them at my grandfather's memorial. Death. A beautiful holy thing.

We are terrified of it.

We don't talk about it.

We don't ask our parents for their plans.

We ignore the biggest elephant in the room.

We are all dying.

Is this morbid? Maybe and also...healing. Accepting. Allowing. Maybe that is death, too.

Maybe what we are actually afraid of is the grief that accompanies death. The grief that swallows us whole in sadness and sorrow. In the why me's, why now. How am I going to get through this? Alone. Unable to shed light on the darkness that is consuming. Unable to allow light. That deep sticky grief.

Death. A beautiful, holy thing.

I've died a thousand deaths already, overcome losses and fear to break through, back to the land of the living. I am not saying I am not afraid of death. I am. I panic at the thought of having Alzheimer's. I have this unrealistic pressure to work faster and harder just in case my life is cut short. Fear of that unknown. And in the same breath, I am willing to welcome that grief in a little closer to learn from it. To feel it. To allow it to be present, even on the days that it consumes me. To know, no matter how dark it may feel, there is always light. Learning to slow down just a bit, not build like I only have 20 years left. Taking notice of when I feel the pressure & reminding myself I have time. I have plenty of time in the world to do what I love, a mantra I've used for a few years now in the context of being busy, but it works just the same here in reminding of that said time.

There are some great analogies to the process of change from the natural world. The metamorphosis of butterflies, snakes shedding skins, hermit crabs outgrowing their shells and finding new ones. Each of them speaks to aspects of grief but I am really drawn to the example of lobsters. If they survive all their predators, their aging process is so incredibly slow that one of the only reasons they die is due to not having the energy to molt. Think of grief as a shell encasing us, slowing us down, limiting our growth and ability to flourish. I imagine the lobster may think it's dying when trying to shed the old shell. Gratitude is the light, the energy that allows us to eventually release the old shell and embrace the soft new version of ourselves that incorporates the learnings from that season of grief.

I am not encouraging you to make death the new topic at the dinner table, but I am encouraging you to reflect on what you are afraid of. What if death is part of our everyday life? What if we begin to think about the things we choose to let go of as small deaths. We can practice experiencing and processing grief when we grieve the end of relationships, the end of seasons, the habits and patterns that no longer serve us.

I've mourned in the midst of my own becoming. I've grieved the suffering I have endured at the hands of another. I've prayed harder and harder and harder. Those were a thousand deaths. You too have died. You have let go. You have mourned and grieved your own becoming. The question, who in the hell am I and what am I doing with my life. Can that be death too?

I've seen healers, astrologers, therapists, akashic readers, craniosacral practitioners, healing touch professionals. Each time I experience loss, let go, release, I have always been willing to put myself back together with more and new practices to support me.

Do the work. Put yourself back together. Accept what is, and know that you understand more than you did yesterday. From that you can make change. Stop belittling yourself for what you didn't know when you made that choice. You are here now and if you know better, you can do better.

Can you release the fear or the hurt? You don't have to hold on to it. How long do you want to drag that story around behind you? A breakup, a bad relationship with your mom, assault or not getting the promotion. Breathe, allow yourself to feel your emotions. You have survived every thing that's happened in the past and can shed the old shell to allow for new growth this time too.

Can we learn how to face grief with an open heart instead

of wearing a suit of armor and holding a shield? Instead of a battle to be won, what if grief could be a journey of self compassion and empathy?

When my mom was dying I wrote. I wrote. I wrote. I wrote. I put it all down somewhere. I put it all here for you to read. Throughout this book I share writing I did while processing the grief.

None of those writings were for you. They were for me.

Creating work I believe in, gathering women, being a safe landing space, building my vision, is an honor and one I do not take lightly but these words, these writings, these reflections have always been for me. My art of emptying. I think if I hadn't emptied I would not have been able to move on. Stop carrying it all: the wounds, the burdens, the regrets, the guilt. It's a gift that I am brave enough to share here with you. Thank you for allowing me space to share these words.

Yet, I know now that these words are also for you. For us. Those writings gave me permission to understand grief in a new way. They gave me lessons and insights and expansions. They gave me hope. They can give us all hope.

I've heard comments like:

I didn't know death could look that way.

You gave me permission to grieve my own mother's death.

Thank you for sharing your journey so I can have courage in mine. I have finally forgiven my mom.

My writings during that time were holy. They gave us all permission to see that death is part of every day. We are so busy worrying about being stuck versus actually living.

Please, tell me what sparks joy in you? And how often do you have those experiences? Make time and space for joy. Please do not let life keep passing you by.

Today, let's choose to live. Let's find joy in the mundane. Let's have a gratitude practice and see the true abundance we have every single day. Let's not take our breath for granted again. Gratitude finds joy. When was the last time you thought, "Wow, I have clean drinking water." I am assuming if you are reading this you most likely do. And that reminds me that many don't.

Perhaps acknowledging your home, warm water, plants that line the window sill, chairs around a table where you share meals brings you joy. When did we lose sight of those little things? This practice is bringing those things back into focus. Back to your heart.

On March 9th, my mom and dad went to the dentist, and while in the chair, my mom had a massive heart attack.

I remember that call.

"Rach, something's wrong. Get here...I don't know, I don't know...She blacked out in the chair, they didn't know...They started performing CPR..."

The actions of the team at the dentist's office and how close they were to the hospital gave us six more months with Mary.

A miracle.

Starting CPR. Calling 911. Being so damn close to the hospital.

We got to have last moments and memories.

A miracle. A time to celebrate and say goodbye.

A time where we could either be afraid of death or be willing to live fully with the time we had left. The moments we hold on to that may define parts and pieces and how it all slowly fades away. Nothing matters more than being able to have just one more moment.

That day it all shifted for me. Alzheimer's. Death. Mom. Heart attack.

Hi all,

This is the best/easiest way to update.

Yesterday my mom suffered a cardiac arrest. The paramedics were able to get a pulse and get her to the hospital. She is currently going through a hypothermia treatment to let her body and brain rest. They will start warming her back up this evening.

Right now our needs are minimal - we need prayers. We need a miracle for our Mary.

Thank you community for your love, prayers, and support. So many of you have been loved by my mom as she never met a stranger. She is a special one. As the nurses removed each one of her many bracelets we all laughed, she was still sharing her joy.

Thank you!

Update: Tuesday 7:30 pm

They will start the rewarming process this evening. Pray that she stays stable through the night.

Tomorrow they will work to continue to find out what happened and why.

We have no real answers yet except God works miracles every day.

Thanks to everyone who's provided food. Thank you Heather for loving my babies tonight.

Thank you to everyone who's commented on this post, we've enjoyed reading so much love as we sit and wait.

Tonight as my dad and I sat in her room we spoke of one of the greatest gifts she's given to us - the gift of presence. As her mental state has declined she always was Here Now. So giving that gift to you all now - Be Here Now. It's truly all that we have.

Thank you all for wrapping us all up in a big love blanket, we've all felt and appreciated it.

This post started it all for me, the very real process of grieving my mom in a new way.

I couldn't be afraid of her dying any longer because I didn't want to miss a day of her living. I had to accept that in 2016 when diagnosis of early onset Alzheimer's hit - she was dying, so how do I make the most out of her time still alive.

In order to be present, I was thinking about:

How am I not living?

How am I sitting here in my muck?

How am I practicing gratitude?

How am I loving myself and my people deeper?

Let's not take another day for granted.

So often on my gratitude lists I constantly come to this:

I am so grateful to be here. ALIVE, at this moment. Experiencing real things. I am here.

Most of the time, I weep as I write that. I feel what a gift it is to be here. A mom of three, wife to a man who loved me to the best of his ability, daughter to incredible parents, leader, community advocate, gratitude junkie. I am here.

The breath. The holy breath I get to take. I get to slow down and feel the warmth over my top lip in that long slow exhale. I get to slow down and feel my heartbeat in my chest. I get to slow down and feel my belly rise and expand as I fill my lungs so full of air. I get to do that.

We are so busy worrying that we forget how holy each breath is.

Less worrying, more breathing. Less worrying, more living.

Don't be afraid of your drive for more, but make sure you acknowledge what you have. Start gratitude today. It shows you that, in fact, you already have enough of everything.

Being grateful for each item, each moment, each connection allows for abundance to be present and to slow the yearning of "what can be."

I am grateful for:

1.

2.

3.

4.

5.

Today's Update: Isn't prayer amazing? We've felt each one. They are lifting us up. So please keep them coming.

Here's what we do know:

They're weaning her further off sedation.

The neurologist pinched her finger and she winced.

She's opening her eyes and today turned her head to find our voices.

No one's saying too much yet, living day to day is a good thing.

They will start to wean down the ventilator, they tried this morning and she wasn't ready.

Keep praying:

See her brain as healed.

See her heart continue to beat.

See her pain free and at peace.

See her in the divine, trusting the process and the road that is in front of us.

Today because we're being fed on so many levels, I thought I'd add a poem my dad wrote for my mom. And sweet Mary, my goodness how many she has fed.

Fed

She ties yellow flowers
To the tassels hanging
From the cloth

That covers her table
She lights any
Number of candles
Everything in this way
Is imbued with a soft glow
The color of sunlight
Seen through thick honey
And the sweetness of her
Comes through without
Hardness or rejection
And everyone who comes
To her table in this way is fed

The Palace of Flowers by Gerry Grubbs (Dos Madres Press)

Thank you all, friends, family, community, strangers - thank you. It's a gift to be so entangled in all this love. There is a meal train and it's already filled up, as we take this day by day, we will continue to share needs. The food has been such a gift and has truly helped us. Much love!

How can I be afraid of death when the doorbell is ringing for my sweet mom to come home? How can I hold hope any longer? My mom had been gone for some years now. Was this really the way she's leaving us? Just like that. No more time. No more breath. No more new memories.

Death. A beautiful, holy thing.

We aren't the "Yes, take extreme measures to keep her alive" style of folks. The medical team came in to speak with my dad and me, who were the first ones at the hospital. I remember the look in my dad's eyes; he didn't realize what they were saying. They proposed an insane hypothermia treatment saved for the worst of the worst cases. A last hope of treatment. No promises made. Machines and tubes keeping a human alive. She was a shell, dancing between heaven and earth. I knew he wasn't ready to say goodbye, we were holding on to this thread of hope. So we both nodded and said, "Try it. Please just try it."

My mind was swirling with questions:
Who do we need to call?
Who should come in?
Who should know and how much do we say?
Then my aunt and uncle showed up to help, support & feed us on every level.

The bereavement cart was wheeled out—like pretzels and a coke will help solve this. The look in the nurse's eyes exploded with empathy and I am so sorry.

Death. A beautiful, holy thing.

What is important at that moment? What does it all mean? And why does it all matter?

Family sitting vigil from sunrise to sunset. Holding on to the slipperiest sliver of hope. Maybe she will wake up and give us one more day.

Strange how a cardiac arrest accelerated everything. Her dying was now active.

We had to face it.
We had to be afraid and show up anyway. We had to lean in.
We had to ask for help.
We had to pray.
We had to keep on living.

Death. A beautiful holy thing.

These musings kept me afloat in that liminal space:

We can keep memories and keep being afraid of living or…

We can keep memories and start living our full and brilliant lives.

No more death beds.

No more I wish I could've, I should've.

No more waiting.

No more perfect conditions.

I still hold on to that from my own mother. Her wishes and wants and desires. Even though she did so much, she never stopped wanting more, she just was unsure how to get there.

I remember her words from my early twenties, "I wish I would have done that. Oh shoot, I could have done that. Oh, why didn't I think of that?" Those words rang through my bones the day my daughter was born. I knew that when Rosalee was born I could tell her to make her dreams come true or I could get to work on building my own dreams, showing her it's possible.

I started my first company when she was five and a half months old. I strapped her to my back and hand rolled graham crackers. I knew my purpose was to spread the message of gratitude, so I wrapped it around that cookie and gave it a shot.

I didn't want to say those same words to my daughter. The shoulds were being replaced with I don't know but I will show up and figure it out. The why didn't I's were being replaced with yes I can.

I didn't know how, but it wasn't about knowing how. It wasn't about knowing when, just starting. Starting with where you are with what you have.

Money or fear or lack of a business plan wasn't going to stop me from starting. I asked, I asked for help, I asked for guidance, I asked stores to carry my product, I asked friends to come help me pack up cookies. Entrepreneurship pushed me to ask more, to expand my dreams, to do something bigger than myself.

I wanted my daughter to know that the world is her oyster and she too could do anything she dreams of. She too could make the impossible possible. She too could live fully anchored in her own beliefs in the way that she would want to make the world better.

My mom made the world a better and brighter place. She did the work she needed to do and maybe I just picked up where she left off.

I dedicate everything I've built to my mom. Her fearlessness, her desire, her boundless love. It's a huge part of why I was brave enough to step into my own power, my own desires and not be afraid to go after them. My mother, the muse, her sacrifices became my freedoms.

Death. A beautiful, holy thing.

I am grateful for death. I am grateful for grief. I am grateful for my grandfather. I am grateful for my grandmother. I am grateful for my relationships. I am grateful for my mother. I am grateful for my father. I am grateful for beginnings. I am grateful for endings. I am grateful for the inhale. I am grateful for the exhale. I am grateful for every time I have come back to life.

And again, for you. The practice of gratitude.
This book, it's a tool to begin. It's a tool to continue.

I am grateful for:

1.

2.

3.

4.

5.

6.

7.

8.

9.

10.

Sesame Noodles

This recipe is probably the most made recipe of my life. It's easy, quick & is always a favorite at potlucks. I also always make a double batch of sauce so I just wrote it as that. Stick the extra in your fridge and make a quick stir fry or something later this week with it. You're welcome.

Sauce:

1/2 cup Braggs Aminos (you can use soy sauce or coconut aminos, I am a Braggs gal myself)
4 tbs sugar
8 cloves garlic, peeled
4 tbs rice vinegar
6 tbs sesame oil
6 tbs olive oil
1 inch piece of fresh ginger (you can peel it, I don't - more fiber maybe?)

Add all ingredients to your little blender and blend it up. If you don't have a blender I'd mince the garlic & ginger and then just stir it all together.

Noodles:

1 1.50-2oz pack of rice noodles (spaghetti also works great here!)

Veggies:

This is where it can get fun! What's in the fridge? My go-to combo is:

1/2 red onion, sliced
1 head of broccoli, trimmed to florets
3 carrots, sliced
1 cup frozen peas

Instructions:

Cook noodles per package directions.
Sauté veggies in 1 tbs olive oil. This isn't a fussy dish & because I make this on nights that I am rushing I most likely just throw it all in a skillet and cook. I add 1-2 tbs of the sauce in to help cook the veggies.

Once noodles are cooked, drain & rinse (in cold water).

Add to pot, add veggies & sauce according to how saucey you like it. I usually use 3/4 of this batch.

Eat & enjoy.

Want to add protein? Cook your protein of choice how you like it and add it in the mix!

three

The Releasing

March 13, 2020

Patience. What a wonderful word. A big deep breath. Exhale. Feel that calm.

The world right now is just moving faster than we know, but in its swift moments, it's actually creating space for all of us for stillness. The exhale.

I've been watching/listening/reading in the Cardiac ICU fog this week.

A lot of gifts presenting themselves that we can be too busy to see—presence, healing, grief, leaning in, slowing down. These are gifts for us all if we can calm down enough to pick them up.

We too are leaning in for patience.
Patience for the docs and nurses.
Patience for healing. Patience for ventilators.
Patience for heart beats. Patience.
Good things take time.

I encourage us during this down time we've been gifted to call your parents, take cookies to the neighbors, call a friend.

We need connection.

Today's update:
They are working to get the breathing tube out, what progress. Changing meds to continue to wake her up.

They've got her off the fentanyl and onto a lighter drug for comfort. She will follow the sound of your voice.

Today's prayer:
For patience. For clarity. For the divine to continue to guide and nurture us.

And a reminder - support your small businesses during this time. If ordering in, do so through locally owned spots, buy gift cards, and hoard all the Grateful Graham's you can!

As always:
Wash your hands
Order Chinese or ethnic food (they're being hit hard)
Pray for Mary
Stay safe
Love your neighbor
Be kind

I often thought of my mom's younger self while she was passing. She was born in the middle of fourteen kids. They lived in Honeybee, Kentucky, a tiny community near Cumberland Falls. The stories of walking to school uphill both ways, no running water, the outhouse and water moccasins. There were moments and memories she never processed, never healed from. She loved her way through them. She would open some doors, but others remained closed. I know she always did the best she could with what she had. With each of us kids being raised so far apart, she healed more with each one of us. She loved each of us the best that she could with the tools she had in the time with each of us. As a mom of three, I see myself doing the same thing, healing more with each kid. Healing takes time. That has been one of the most empowering lessons to learn, believe and share.

Our parents may not have done "our best" but they did their best. They did the best that they could with the tools they were given. They did the best they could with their own grief or generational wounds. And now I am doing my best with my kids with the tools I have, and I am always growing.

She moved out of Honeybee to find work when she was a teenager.

My paternal great grandfather opened a restaurant in the 40's called The Country Kitchen. My dad's dad worked there and was a good Kentucky boy. He hired nearly all of my mom's family when they came here in search of work. They were all hard workers. It's also where my mom first laid eyes on my dad—the owner's grandson. They all told her that she wasn't good enough for him, she was just a poor country bumpkin, and he was too good for her. She leapt anyway. She knew she was worthy of being with the owner's grandson, and love is love.

My parents loved each other for more than forty three years. They healed and grew together. They fought and forgave. They were willing to open their own hearts and do their own healing as best as they could for themselves and then rippled that out to us.

May we all hold our worthiness like Mary did. Go after the person of your dreams. Go after the job of your dreams. Go after the freedom your heart is calling for.

After her heart attack, we were frozen in time waiting for updates and the progress that would allow us to take her home. The world was changing, and I barely noticed. There wasn't room for the outside world when my own world was crumbling. It was too much so I chose her, I chose my mom and I would choose her again.

I remember looking at my kids two weeks into our COVID-19 lockdown and quite blankly saying, "Why are you not at school?"

I was so focused on my mother, this new space, the transition, the work of managing next steps.

I had been mourning for years, but my dad was just beginning his final goodbyes to the woman he loved so intently, the woman many of his poetry books are dedicated to, the woman who would take care of everything without so much as a sigh.

So I did my best to manage her care, setting up hospice, doctor appointments, and communications. I wanted my dad to be present with her without the stress of managing her final days, my gift to him in those last few months. At the same time, I was managing my own house, my companies, and my parents' home in a lot of ways (meal delivery, teaching my dad to do laundry, soaking up any moment I could with her).

I remember the day my dad said, "Sell your house and move in. I want you to buy this house anyway, and well, you are doing too much. Let's be together, simplifying it for everyone."

We moved into their house before the school year started to make it as smooth as possible for the kids, and we were able to be present in her last ten weeks of life.

Moving into this house saved my life. My mom dying saved my life.

Did 2020 show up and dump the biggest bucket of grief into our laps or what? It came in and took over, we were stranded at home with no context for what was happening in the world, swallowed by fear and death and grief and the unknown.

Nowhere to go. No way to understand what was happening. No idea when or if it will ever end. Two weeks turned into two years and we were still engulfed in grief, trying to get "back to normal." Our friends died. Our family members died. Our kids' schools shut down and mothers and fathers became teachers overnight. Going to work became an exercise in how to turn a corner into an office. Human touch was just out of reach. Hearts ached for connection. Fear controlled conversations.

The deaths of Breonna Taylor and George Floyd shook us to our core. Grief drenched us, and we didn't have the tools to wring it out.

How do we have gratitude for a pandemic? I have a lot of gratitude for it, because it allowed me to be present in a way I never could have imagined before. It gave me time as a small business owner to slow down so I could help manage the care of my mom.

Are we afraid of dying? Or are we afraid of living?

Did the pandemic help us learn that answer any clearer?

Are we going to carry the grief of the last few years or are we going to learn how to process it? Sit it down. Talk about it. Release it.

How do we release it? How do we talk about it? How do we feel about all of that?

In 2021, I developed Head to Heart Mentoring, a program about dropping from your head to heart, clearing out some clutter, grief, and allowing you to step fully into who you feel called to become. The first homework I usually assign, especially when we are dealing with grief, is to write a letter to their littlest self.

See, this grief, it's not from the pandemic, at least not all of it. It's generational. It's lessons we have been taught, the way our parents spoke to us, trauma, decades of choices, fear of being seen, and lack of belief in our ability to be the change.

So, in this moment, again, take a big deep breath. Get into your body. Slow down. And another.

Now set a timer for sixty seconds. In this stillness, can you see yourself as a child, the moments some of those lessons or grief occurred?

When you were seven and being told that you "can't do more than one thing."

When you were four and your "stepdad told you you were fat."

When you were twelve and "your mom reminded you you'd never be able to do that thing."

When you were nine and your parents divorced.

I believe that is where we need to trace our grief back to.

See your younger self, the way your hair fell, the dirt on your palms from playing outside, your favorite outfit you loved to rock and now laugh at—how did I ever think that outfit was cool?

See your younger self. Smell, feel, remember, breathe. Don't be afraid. Remember you are safe.

I think this is one of the most powerful forms of healing we as humans can do. Remembering, opening those doors you've closed or nailed shut. Remembering the hurt and allowing it to be present, but also allowing yourself to acknowledge and hopefully release.

I've been practicing this form of retracing, a spiritual practice, since my early twenties.

I've written letters, probably hundreds. Letters to little Rachel, letters to mean girls and women, letters of pain and letters of forgiveness, letters of hope and dreams and desires. Letters of why me, letters of thank God it was me.

I wrote so many letters to the little girl who never felt good enough, my value was only found in being good and working harder than anyone else. Now, through deep healing I am still writing letters but finally acknowledging the girl who experienced her own traumas and struggled to find her place in the world. I write for the girl whose marriage was something different than what she thought or expected it to be.

Letters about all I want to release so I can have more joy.

Less suffering, more joy. Less pain, more abundance.

I think this practice is powerful. I give it for homework often in my consulting or mentoring, in my business lectures, and in my one-on-one's with strangers who feel safe enough to tell me their story.

These letters take time; healing takes time. I am willing to get in the trenches with my pain because I know it's the only way to liberation. I tried to numb myself out for a long time. I numbed with work and kids, wine and food. I became a master at going numb. I am currently writing a letter to that little girl too, who did her best as she tried to manage so much pain at once—being the main provider for her family, for the smallness she felt in her marriage and tried to pray her way out of, for being so sad she couldn't call her mom and tell her all about it. I am putting it all here so bluntly. The filters have been removed, for the first time in a very long time, I can see clearly.

I am no longer numb, I am no longer afraid. I am finally safe. And as hard as these words may be to write I am also sure they will be hard to read, but they are my truths. I know how to speak the truth, I know how to be vulnerable, and I know that I am not alone in my suffering.

I suffered in our marriage. I thought that to be a good wife, I was supposed to do whatever he wanted and not what I wanted or needed. Every ask or need I had came with a cost. In hindsight I poured my pain into my work, constantly seeking the light, I worked harder and harder. If my telling my truth helps one woman understand what is happening in her life, recognize her strength and helps her find her voice, I will say it over and over again. One truth to save one life is worth every letter that is being typed right now.

A spiritual teacher and therapist was the main person I confided in. I stayed in the marriage for so long because she would tell me to PRAY HARDER. I trusted her, she knew "better" because she was a licensed professional. She told me that when the women heal, the men will follow suit. I was feeling defeated in my marriage daily and being told by my therapist that my husband would be so beautiful on the other side; to keep praying. Looking back on it now, her words enabled him and kept me caged.

We can do hard things. We can endure pain and suffering. We can lose ourselves, lose our voice, and lose our ability... AND we can heal, we can unlearn, we can find our voice. This book is me finding my voice. These words are me healing on a cellular level along with the help of many incredible healers, therapists, and practitioners. Through dying and coming back to life.

So I offer this practice to you here, in this book. I want you to know that no matter what you are going through and as alone as you may feel, YOU ARE NOT ALONE. You are not alone. You are worthy and able to start anew, to heal, to find yourself again. No matter if it was a "big T" trauma or a "little t" trauma. You don't have to keep carrying it.

Be grateful for what it taught you, and be willing to let it go.

Now let's take this into action. Write your younger self a letter. I've even left a few pages blank for you in this chapter to draft one. I encourage you, perhaps not today but this week, to write. Don't let this practice pass you by. Even if you had a "great, non traumatic, everything is sooooo fine life" I assume you still have some memories or moments to release. Please just give yourself time to feel them.

In the letter, I want you to write about and acknowledge the pain then write every beautiful, positive thing about this younger you.

Here's an example:

Dear little self,

THANK YOU. I want you to know that I love you. So often you have questioned your worth & felt lonely. You are not alone sis, I promise. You diminish your light because you never want to over shadow anyone, you often think you are too much & stress about the impact. You are doing enough. You have permission to take up more space. You have had experiences you would wish upon no one, and you survived every single one of them. You are strong. You are safe. I am sorry you went through those things. You didn't deserve that and you listened & let yourself heal. Be proud of that. Thank you for your tenderness and loving heart. I am so sorry you feel scared right now. You are enough. You are not ugly or fat, you are so beautiful. You are so beautiful. You are doing big things. You are brave and creative. You dream so big people don't even understand how you do it all. You are kind and generous and here at eleven years old, you are enough. No matter what they are saying. You are enough. I am so proud of you for how you live your life with love and gratitude and compassion. Keep going.

Love,
Me

I think this practice is so important because we are flailing through our lives, riddled with worry and anxiety and suffering. But we don't have to live like that any more. We can embody our fullness and live each day in joy. Even with pain. Even when our rights get taken away. Even in suffering. I am not a victim but a survivor. I have built incredibly beautiful, bold businesses alongside my suffering. Even in pain, I didn't stop trying to find a way to live.

I want you to be alive. Fully.

Once you write this letter, read it. Feel it. Grieve with it. See your inner child as safe and secure. In my opinion, once you feel safe, once your inner child feels safe, then can you be in your body, grounded and ready to look at the next piece.

I still find myself writing letters to little Raybird (my nickname and the name of a favorite cocktail recipe included in this book for you). You can never write too many letters. Let it come out. You don't have to choose to keep carrying this all through your days. I often imagine these stories that I'm carrying as a big ball & chain around my ankle, clink clanking as I scurry through my day, hitting walls and pulling me back, always fighting that energetic force of living and grieving.

Do something about it.
Allow yourself to put it down in writing.
Allow yourself to be seen and loved.
Allow yourself time and space to love yourself deeper.
You are enough. And I am so grateful you are here with us
  right now.

Gratitude got me through the pandemic. Gratitude got me through my mother's death. Gratitude got me through the dissolution of my marriage. Gratitude got me here putting these words down. Gratitude helped me burst through the fear.

Remember - gratitude never says, "Oh, do not be afraid you silly." It says, "It's ok, you are safe; you may feel afraid but take a breath—look, you have water, shoes on your feet, a roof over your head, do not be afraid and remember you are safe." It's reminding you of your fullness. It gets you out of fight or flight and into your body. Stop the flight. Breathe. Practice. Be afraid. Love more. There can never be too much love. There can never be too much gratitude.

Dear Littlest Self,

You are enough. You are so kind and beautiful.

♥

♥

♥

Love,

(please sign & date)

My goal is to embody those two words - love + gratitude.

My goal is to remain soft and strong. A balance of feminine and masculine.

My goal is to love my own enoughness; which I still struggle with. I've recently been working with a coach and still processing where I don't believe in myself enough. How I am still afraid to step into my own greatness. Those voices I still carry with me. You are too big. You are too loud. You are too much. You have too much going on. How do you do it all? You? Why you? Why not me? Tears still stream down as I write those words, reminding me that I still have love to wrap around them.

And I do that like this.

I am grateful for my voice, may I continue to use it to voice love and joy. Be loud. The world needs all of you.

I am grateful for my body. My big hips, Grubbs thighs that rub and wiggle as I walk through my day, birthed three incredible babies.

I am grateful for my visions and dreams. To work towards goals with love in my heart and gratitude in my fingers. I can do anything.

I am grateful to be here in this moment, ME, soaking up moments and memories, bad days and good days.

I am worthy of anything I desire.

I am grateful for my busy, for my businesses. I have all the time in the world to do what I love.

What is your negative self-talk?

What bubbles up for you as you read these words? What does your heart say?

Take a few minutes, breathe, you are safe. Negative thoughts:

♥

♥

Now rewrite them wrapped in light, love, and gratitude:

♥

♥

Do you feel that lightness, that shift of energy? Do you feel wrapped in a golden bubble of light, seeing how new things are possible? How you are wanted and needed here? How loved you are? How worthy of living life you are? How you too can practice gratitude for every moment? I am so proud of you. These pages dug in a little deeper, but I don't think I can write a book on grief or gratitude and not share my practices.

It is what I believe. It is what I practice. It is what I teach.

You are worthy.
You are good enough.
You deserve your boldest desires.

Prayer for a gentle week:

May we see enough in our enoughness

May each day be touched by grace

May we find good in the simple things and remember what brings us joy

More joy this week For me & for you

Stop & smell the roses, remove your mask, take in that tender smell

Remember it For it is holy Like me & you

May your heart smile

As you teach, clean, cook, be

May you be whole this week

Your wholeness a gift, your truest you

Like me & you

The Raybird

1.5 oz rum
1 oz Campari
1/2 lime
1 oz simple syrup
3 oz pineapple juice
Sparkling water

Now, I am sure you can shake this or stir it or however fancy you want to get it, but this practical patty does it just like this...

Rum in my glass. Add Campari. Squeeze that 1/2 lime right in there. Add your simple syrup & pineapple juice. Stir it. Add a few ice cubes and top with sparkling water.

Make it non alcoholic by skipping the rum & Campari. When I do this I like to use coconut La Croix because it's like a tropical paradise.

four

The Forgiveness

A friend, recently divorced, said to me, "I don't think I can forgive him," and a deep conversation into what forgiveness looks like followed.

I think we've been taught that forgiveness is overlooking bad behavior or unhealthy patterns.

Forgiveness for me is keeping my side of the street clean. It's looking at my part, my humanness, how I showed up. Forgiveness is not forgetting, it's just releasing the burden instead of carrying it with you everywhere you go. It's seeing that everyone is human, everyone has a story, and they are showing up with that if they are not doing that work, the healing work that these pages share. The inner knowing of what's good, being helpful, practicing kindness.

Even now, during my own time in the trenches working toward forgiveness I understand it will take time, but it allows me to process the full extent of the experience. I am not sure I have fully forgiven my ex-husband. I know that for full healing and forgiveness, I need to be able to acknowledge and process those nights I spent laying wide awake, afraid, suffering. I have to find a way through to be able to forgive the whole, not just parts of it. I want to forgive him, for my own heart's sake, for my kids' sake, for not wanting to carry the burden with me any longer. I am working toward forgiveness, each memory or nightmare I am one step closer. I am proud of myself. I am running towards forgiveness, I want to free myself of the burden of this pain. Facing it is the only way I know how. I'm so close, because I am so happy, every day an absolute miracle.

I loved him, my ex-husband. I fell in love with his stories and his big hands, the way I used to feel safe with him. My heart shattered going through divorce because I believe so deeply in the sanctity of marriage. I witnessed my parents in love, I witnessed my dad loving his wife through death and knew that I wasn't going to have that experience either. I've forgiven myself for not knowing or seeing what was really happening in my marriage. I've also forgiven him in a lot of ways for being unable to get the help he needed. I know he did the best he could but now I know he stopped trying to do that best a long time ago and that's what maybe hurt the most. The man I loved gave up while I kept fighting, trying to save us for so long. It's been incredibly empowering to spend this time actually finding myself again, making me whole, no longer laying awake but sleeping soundly.

I am no longer numb, I am no longer afraid.

The Greater Good Science Center at Berkeley, which studies the psychology, sociology and neuroscience of well being, says psychologists generally define forgiveness as "A conscious, deliberate decision to release feelings of resentment or vengeance toward a person or group who has harmed you, regardless of whether they actually deserve your forgiveness."
(https://greatergood.berkeley.edu/topic/forgiveness/definition)

Forgiveness is not merely accepting what happened or ceasing to be angry. Rather, it involves a voluntary transformation of your feelings, attitudes, and behavior, so that you are no longer dominated by resentment and can express compassion, generosity, or the like toward the person who wronged you.

Here is one of my biggest lessons on forgiveness and how it shaped who I am. It's one of my most vulnerable stories, one I've carried for over two decades now. I am so proud to share this story with love and gratitude.

I was raised in a loving home, the middle child of a middle class family. I went to school and got good grades. I loved being the funny one, the loud one, and the good one. And if you know me I still love being all of those things today, too.

I never wanted to rock the boat. I had an older sister who rocked enough boats, so I thought if I could just be so good, get through school, go to law school, and work alongside my dad, my life would be perfect. Maybe not perfect, because I knew perfection wasn't real, but good. Good felt real. Maybe some of that was an unspoken expectation. My expectation, my need to not let anyone down. Funny how expectations can really wreck our world. Expectations we have for ourselves. Expectations we have for others

Do good.
Do right.
Don't let anyone down.

Phew—that is a lot, right?

So instead of doing good, doing right and not letting anyone down, I got pregnant. I was a senior in high school, at an all girl Catholic high school nonetheless.

I broke my dad's heart the day I told him.

I realized later, as I worked through this experience, that I broke mine too.

In a knee jerk reaction my parents asked me to move out. I did. A senior in high school, a small part-time job, no partner.

I first moved into a home for unwed mothers, which lasted three to four weeks. They wanted me to quit school and work for the church. I remember the room, large with bad wallpaper; the big ugly floral kind from the 80's. All over. Brown carpet. Small beds. Old wooden bedside tables. Space to fit maybe a suitcase worth of belongings. Beds lined up like you'd picture, like in Little Orphan Annie perhaps. No privacy, just lost women who somehow found their way there hoping to be saved or to find redemption or just simply have a roof over their heads.

I drove to school every day, about forty minutes each way. They didn't like that. I remember feeling so much shame for trying to finish my high school education. I remember calling my parents and asking them to please let me come home. The church didn't want me there and they wanted to take away my education. That couldn't happen.

Luckily, my parents let me move back home; partially because the new place I was going to move to would let me move in just a few weeks. I had to be 18 to live there. So I moved home for a few weeks, and a day or two after my eighteenth birthday, my mom moved me into the next center for unwed mothers. This one was different. The folks that ran it were kind and helpful, they had a lot of resources and a deep belief that it was all going to be ok. I had my own apartment, and there was a common area and a curfew, but I had my own space to be in. I still continued to commute to my high school, a bit closer this time, only thirty minutes. It was good; it was okay. I was safe. I knew it wasn't forever, and that it was where I needed to be right then.

I stayed there for about four months. I graduated high school then I went to work and drove home to my apartment. It was weird. But I was safe.

That summer, still pregnant, I finally called my parents. I spoke to my mom all the time, but my dad and I didn't speak to each other the entire time I was pregnant. I told my mom, "I need to come home." Maybe it was nesting, but nothing I was doing was making that space really feel like home. So, I moved back home in the mid August heat, just a few weeks before I was due. I was so grateful to be back in my purple bedroom where I had hand-stenciled flowers around the door, with my futon and a crib next to it. I was just a little girl, trying to do big things.

I had decisions to make, hard choices, but giving up Camden...I couldn't. I was grateful to be back where it was familiar.

Grateful to be back where I belonged. Grateful to be home. I stayed there until Camden was six months old then we went back out on our own, forging our new life together.

Maybe the miracle the entire time was this lesson of forgiveness.

For nine months my dad and I didn't speak. There was no congrats on your graduation, I love you, or any other words muttered. Now, being on this side of it I couldn't imagine trying to live with someone and not speak to them, but for us that was what it was for that time.

Another reason this time was difficult for me was because at 18, my dad had a son who was given up for adoption. I was eight the first time I remember seeing my dad cry. His son turned eighteen and he told us about him. I witnessed him mourn a child he wished he had known. Luckily, Dan was looking for my dad. They were looking for each other. We've seen Dan and his family every year since then.

Maybe that's why adoption wasn't an option for me. I had seen first hand the pain it caused. I was supposed to go to law school or maybe become a doctor. But really, law school was the plan because then I could work with my dad. But the moment he found out about my pregnancy, all of his expectations were shattered. Just like mine. I think he was grieving; he gave up on the future he thought I was going to have. I love my dad. I know he did his best and was working through his own pain.

For whatever reason, my heart always offered forgiveness to my dad. I knew when I told him, when our hearts shattered together, that he had to heal his heart and I had to heal mine. I couldn't try to heal his. I couldn't fix this. I couldn't make this just go away. We needed that space. That time. That silence.

In that silence, what I found was forgiveness. Human to human forgiveness. Deep forgiveness.

This forgiveness said, "I see you hurting, and I know I hurt you.

I can't fix the hurt, but I can help you let go of how you feel it 'should be.'"

I am a fixer, I love finding a solution and I know sometimes the only solution is time and space. It's allowing the liminal space to be present, sitting in the unknown. Feeling hope and hardship at the same time.

I truly can type these words and say a miracle happened. I forgave my father in the midst of teenage angst, pregnancy, being kicked out, not spoken to, lost and alone. I forgave him for how he reacted and how I thought he should react. I forgave him for the silence as I later realized there wasn't a word we could have shared if we had wanted to.

I forgave him because he was doing his best to understand - just like I was. Sure I was crushed, upset, angry, confused, but I knew those emotions were easy to work through—well, maybe not easy but doable. The miracle lay in the forgiveness. How could I ever harbor feelings greater than what he was feeling. I couldn't.

I broke his heart. I broke my heart.

I never blamed him or hated him for how he handled his daughter being seventeen and pregnant.

I knew then that my job was to love and allow him time to heal. How, at seventeen, did I know that or believe it or trust? I had no clue why this was all so clear. Now, I know it was because even then I had gratitude. I know now it's because when I was eleven he told me my work was to fully love myself and not take responsibility for another's words or lack thereof. It was as if in that moment he was those mean girls and my job was to remember that I was enough, that I was worthy of being loved, even if it meant not getting that love from my dad.

The day Camden was born, my parents were out of town and rushed back to be with me. Alongside them, my doula, and other family members, Camden Ray Grubbs was born at 4:26

in the afternoon. A long labor and exhausting birth. A child birthed a child. In that instant, the last nine months vanished, and all we saw was the amazing gift of life. The moment he took his first breath was the moment those silent months vanished, and standing right beside me was my father. He found his way back home just like I did.

I am grateful for this and how gratitude held space for forgiveness.

Gratitude helped me see my dad through a new lens, a human lens. We think forgiveness needs to be, "Well, I will forgive them when they do this or they do that."

That's not forgiveness.

That's ego saying it has to be my way.

For me, forgiveness says, "I will love you for you and be here alongside you as you do your work."

It is not holding a grievance over someone's head until I get the words or actions I need.

What does forgiveness mean to you?

Is there someone in your life you need to forgive?

Where is that taking up space in your body right now? How does it feel?

Is it hard or sharp? Does it feel lumpy and grumpy? Does your breath feel heavy when you are sitting with it?

How do we go a little deeper here?

How do we bring gratitude to hold this space with us?

Let's look at some pieces together, shall we?

So first, tell me, who do you need to forgive?

Write it here:

♥

♥

♥

♥

Forgiving is NOT forgetting.
Forgiving is NOT forgetting.
Forgiving is NOT forgetting.

If you have experienced deep trauma, I am not saying to just forgive them and move on. I am encouraging you to be tender with your heart and look at how you lighten your load.

I don't know that I have forgiven everyone who has hurt me, maybe that's the entangled web of addiction that part of my life has been living in.

Forgiveness is not forgetting. But I do hold hope. Maybe one day.

Unless we do our healing work, we bring our own "stuff" to the table, our wounded self to the forefront of the conversation. We drag around the weight of those unresolved experiences into today. Unless we practice gratitude as fluidly as drinking water and forgiveness as gently as a summer breeze, we are slowing down our ability to grow and love and live in joy.

Forgiveness is stepping into our power using our voice to the fullness we can. It's saying, "I love myself enough, I am ready to have freedom from this pain." We all deserve that freedom.

Now let's answer these questions:

What are you grateful for about a person who has hurt you? Can you come up with at least one thing? If this is a parent, perhaps your gratitude lies with the fact that because of them, you are here. That's a blessing!

What about this situation are you grateful for? Think broadly if you have to. You're healthy, you are alive, you are in a better space now.

How will offering forgiveness create more space and lighten your load? Why share this story now? Much like grief is stored in our body, so is the act of forgiveness.

Grief is that unknown. Grief of a strained relationship. Grief of being a teen mom. Grief of feeling lost and alone. Grief of what now. Grief of plans or expectations being shattered.

What if forgiveness makes space for our grief, allowing us to empty it? Could forgiveness be action for grief? You allow it to be there, the hurt and the pain. But forgiving, an action on your part keeps your side of the street clean.

Forgiveness, accepting what happened to work itself out, to feel safe knowing that I've done my best.

I am grateful I accepted my dad's reaction because it taught me something. It helped me understand another human better. I'm grateful for it because it made me better. I worked hard. I loved more. I had compassion for someone who couldn't have it for themselves. Forgiveness allows that to happen.

Forgiveness allowed me to process grief at seventeen and again more deeply when I was 37 and moved back in with my parents during my mom's final weeks. It was the first time my dad and I really talked about it since Camden's birth.

I also have a son who I am proud of. He graduated college, something he did on his own by working hard in school, getting grants and working in restaurant kitchens around Cincinnati. He is strong. When he hugs me now, he sees me. When he graduated he said, "I know you gave this up for me, this certificate is for us mom. We did this." I wouldn't change one thing about that chapter. As hard as it was to become a mother at eighteen, quit college for work, tuck a toddler into bed every single night alone. I did it.

We did it.

We did this, kid. Yes we did.

April 28, 2020

The lump you wake up with in your throat

The tears while cooking supper

The sorrow in your kids eyes when they are unsure

The anger of why

Exhaustion did I brush my teeth today

Unsure

Confusion

Lack of understanding or motivation

The tears any time any place tears

Zoomed out

The unknown

Grief.

It's ok to call all of these new wild feelings what they are. Grief was not my word for 2020, but I feel like I've spent the last twelve weeks in grief training. It's come and nestled not so gently in my lap. It's painted its name on my walls. It's woken me up in panic. It's called me by name. Grief.

The last seven weeks, yes we are in week seven, I've heard, read, and seen so many folks lost in the newness they are feeling. That's grief. It's ok, too.

See, what I've learned in the last twelve weeks is the power of the grieving process.

Grief will bring you to the edge.

Edge of despair, dismantling, exhaustion. It walks you so closely up to the tip top and I asked to stay there for a bit; to understand, to not shy away from what a gift the grief can be.

It's helped me get to know myself better. It's helped me shed so many unwanted thoughts and feelings. It's made a clearer life I want to live. It's shown me my heart beating gratefully. It's been wonderful and hard and lovely and lonely to sit and understand it.

I could've shoved it. Told it to go away. What is it that we say, oh yes – NO THANKS I AM FINE. I am fine. I'm fine. Nothing's wrong.

There is nothing fine about this.

Friends, this time, this grief. It's ok. It won't last forever, and truth be told, the sooner you sit still and listen to what it's sharing the sooner it will vanish in the night.

We are all grieving something right now. There is loss happening. I guess my point is - how do you want to wake up from this?

You'll wake up one morning and that lump in your throat will be gone and you won't cry in your cereal or be angry at the delivery guy for leaving your box on the neighbor's porch or even upset at yourself for how slow you've let yourself be. The slowness you've given yourself is a gift. It will say "Thank you."

My Favorite Strawberry Smoothie

Ahh, a smoothie recipe. How original. But for real, I love this smoothie. I drank it for months straight & if you know me I am not really a food repeater like that. It was sweet & salty and kept me full and well, I like that combo.

Ingredients:

   1 cup frozen sliced strawberries
   1/2 frozen banana
   1/2 tbs maple syrup (can omit, but I like it)
   1 tbs peanut butter
   1 tsp chia seeds
   1 tsp hemp seeds
   Cover with almond milk or milk of choice

Place all items in your blender.
Mix it, Mix it real good.
Eat & enjoy!

five

The ICU

June 5, 2020

An update

Friends,

My sweet mama has entered into the final stages of her Alzheimer's. Typing those words, there's almost relief and a streaming set of tears. Relief knowing her suffering will soon be over. Tears because my mama's soul will soon be leaving this earth.

I've thought about this entire 2020 year, the world being on fire right now, innocents dying and, I'm so grateful she's not felt the pain of the real world this year. Her gift was loving people, you see, and if we can do anything to carry on her legacy, it's to love more - she didn't care your size, your color, your financial means - she saw YOU, and YOU were always good enough for her.

She taught me one of the greatest lessons this year after a doctor's appointment when she simply said, "Life is love," and I'll forever carry that phrase at the forefront of my work and my life.

We are in a rapid decline phase. It's weird and beautiful. My mother is gone while her physical body still walks beside us. The Veil is thin. Her parents, who died years ago, visit her daily. It's a gift to witness her with a foot in both worlds.

We still think we have months, not weeks left. And that's all dependent on the rate of decline. But the work is truly 24/7 care right now. My family is fully committed to the care it will take for her to have a peaceful transition. Maybe that's my way of asking for grace because I know if she were here she'd want to be on the front lines fighting or at least feeding the people for justice.

If you feel called to help, our biggest need is meals as it's the most "work" for us and keeping up with anything. There's a meal train so at least we can ask for help one to two times a week while my siblings and dad try to handle the rest. If you have questions on the meal train please contact Stephanie.

Pray for my dad. Hold him up right now. Pray for strength as he loses his best friend. Pray for comfort and grace as he takes care of her. Pray for soft hearts living a divine journey.

We've gotten through the last three months (which felt more like six months). Thank you for holding us up right now along with the weight of the world, everyone's shoulders are feeling tired and heavy. It's ok. Take a deep breath. Drop into your heart and keep on marching. It will be a land of milk and honey on the other side!

We've entered the active dying stage. With Alzheimer's, I suppose it's all the dying stage. Seeing my mom slip away like a one ton whale, blubbery and big, all consuming. That dying. That grief. It was different.

I remember the day she was waking up in the hospital, when we spoke with palliative care before moving down from the ICU.

They moved us (kicked us out gently) because Mary is a beast.

She woke up, said enough of this shit, and promptly pulled her central line out of her neck. She said, "I don't need this."

They didn't want to restrain her. Her brain and heart were too fragile.

They moved us out of the ICU, to a regular room. The hospital was preparing for the very first influx of COVID-19 cases and wanted to have as many beds available in specialized units as possible. Bless them, bless you nurses. Seriously, you all are doing God's work; the juggle of beeping machines, broken hearts, questions from a billion family members.

That first night she was in the new room, they gave her some meds for sleeping and we all went home. The next night she was more lucid so I stayed for hours until she fell asleep, and it was in those hours where I remember seeing that dance between life and death begin. The veil becoming so thin. Her mom joined us, and I remember the doe-like face Mom made when she saw her, the face we would all make if we got to see our mom. The face of comfort and safety.

That face that said, "Oh, what a wonderful child I am, Mom is right here reminding me so."

I took a video of her at that moment, and I recently watched it. Her reaching out, the next steps on her journey home. She looked relieved and scared. She looked comforted but unsure. She saw familiar faces, ones she hadn't seen in years, and all the forgetfulness of her disease faded. She remembered who they were, and she was happy to see them.

Her mom died one year & seven days before I was born. I never got to meet Granny but from the stories, I know she was a strong woman, but their relationship was not the easiest. My mom worked through her own pain to arrive at forgiveness knowing that her own mother did the best she could with what she had. In this moment Mom was happy to be reunited with her, to get comfort from her mother like she may never have had in her entire life.

Grief taught me to pay attention, to watch her and that dance, to not be afraid of it. To open up and see how beautiful, how brutal death could be.

How I weep as I type this. It makes me want to hug my littles, to remind them I am doing my best. I work too much, I overthink it and over budget it—we need more money in our fun budget. That I too am doing the best I can with the tools I have.

This path isn't about perfection but perhaps one of understanding. And grace. Loads of grace. I can choose to do better, as I learn more, grow and unlearn things, too.

The unlearning is maybe even more valuable than the learning in some instances.

Death, a beautiful, holy thing.

Acceptance.

Denial.

Grief. Upon grief.

A gift of time.

All in one single breath. That truth shifted. I could feel that my dad knew his wife wasn't going to be here forever. My mom wasn't going to be here forever. Funny how we think our parents are always going to be around, even though we know that they won't be. But that reality coming true was a whole new pill to swallow. I am grateful for this gift of time because I know not everyone has a chance to say goodbye, which has its own beauty and divinity. Both of those experiences are brutiful. Both are grief filled. Both are exhausting on every imaginable plane. Both are hard. There is no perfect way to lose someone, quick or slow.

I found myself wanting to be present, not let one second slip by knowing that I did everything I could to spend time helping and supporting this transition to the best of my ability. I know what a miracle, a true blessing from God that we got our Mary for months not moments.

The day she had her heart attack the nurse asked if we wanted to take extreme measures to keep her alive, but we all needed those last moments, not just our family but this community, you reading these words.

Her miracle of waking up got me here, and for that I am grateful.

How do you celebrate death?
How do you grieve and hold gratitude in the same breath?
How do you witness the miracles of crossing over?
How do you love them through it while also loving yourself?

I am not sure I have the answers to these questions.

Death. I do not want to be afraid of it, and I am nowhere ready for my time to come to an end. But how do we talk about it, how do we feel it, how do we celebrate it?

Every single day I am grateful for every breath.

Celebrating death. Sounds like an oxymoron I guess. For me, celebrating death unfolded as:

Being present

Holding her hand

Playing her favorite songs

Filling wine bottles with grape juice so she could have an unlimited supply of "wine" (that phase lasted about two months and boy did our girl go to town!)

Family celebrations more fun and more consistent than before

Traveling to visit family so they had a chance to see her and be with her before she passed

Seeing that she was still with us - every day a blessing

Celebrating death quite frankly is MAKING THE MOST OUT OF THE TIME WE HAVE.

Holy shit. We let so much time and life pass us by when we should be celebrating our lives every day. Stop taking for granted that you're still here. Celebrate your aliveness.

You guys, there were some really hard days. Days when all we could do was cry. Days where I couldn't visit, I couldn't see her in that state, the suffering, her not remembering my name or my face.

But there were so many days we laughed, when she created "art," when her nurse would come in and she would squeal for joy, when she looked at you and saw you. Days when we could lay in bed next to her and remember doing the same thing when we were young. Here I was mothering my mother.

Being her daughter. Being her mother.

Grief and gratitude, for everything that hurt. I found three things to be grateful for. I pushed myself to lean in, to come back to my practice. To come back to my breath.

I went back to a space where I allowed grief to be in but the same space where I could wrap that grief in light, in gratitude. Did I do this every time? Hell no. Did I do this a lot of the time? Hell yes.

The practice only works if you practice it. I often tell people gratitude is the strongest muscle I have dammit, so let me use it. We can have all of these tools in our tool box but if we never use them, what good are they?

Feel the grief. Stop running.

How does each of us choose to move forward when we are crushed by death, or projects failing or hurtful words or old, untrue judgements? Start living. Is that our new motto? Phew. I am trying. I am trying every day to learn how to feel the grief and be brave enough to live; to find the balance there.

Changing your mom's diapers will invite deep reflection. It made me look at what I am leaving on the table because I am afraid of going after it.

Wondering what they will think? The "Oh Rachel I don't know how you do it all" burden, but if her death taught me anything it's to stop leaving it on the table.

Time is precious and I am no longer going to let my fear or old beliefs around money, worthiness and time hold me back any longer. Her death taught me to live fully, as me, all of me, no longer afraid (still working on that part) but knowing that I have today and I do not want to let it pass me by.

That also means I have to feel it. I have to have my heart shattered and learn to put it back together. It means that I have real, vulnerable conversations with people. It means I have to stop working and go to the pool for eight hours.

During those last few months we had some really good times.

She came back to us in a more deteriorated state, but she got dressed, could find the bathroom, would talk to us, laughed and asked for wine.

If you ever met Mary then you know she blinged. She had bracelets on both arms. I still question how she was ever able to brush her teeth or hair with so much weight. In those last few years you never saw her without everything she could adorn herself with.

She also never shared those treasures. Even as a kid she'd let me try things on and would be like, "ok, let's put that back now." She was proud of her treasures and since my dad never said no to her, she had plenty. I remember taking her to the doctor for an appointment. The nurse, the kindest woman, looked at her and said with childlike joy, "Oh Mary, I just love your bracelets. They are so beautiful."

Mom melted. She was so smitten, she hugged her nurse, told her thank you, and promptly took off a small beaded bracelet and handed it to her.

Witnessing my mom take that bracelet off was something I don't think I had ever seen her do. She shared a lot, but her jewelry was not one of those things. This moment, it cracked me wide open and changed my life. I was both in shock and awe over what was unfolding.

She looked at me in pure joy, pure divine joy, and smiled at the nurse, saying, "You are so beautiful. I am so happy to share with you."

If you knew my mom, you know she was an open hearted, let me feed you kind of woman. Witnessing her unconditional love, feeling that moment, giving that bracelet to a stranger because even while dying, my mom still remembered the feeling of unconditional love.

She looked at me and I said, "Wow mom, that was so nice."

And she promptly stated, "Life is love."

LIFE IS LOVE.

Ahhhh. This dying woman. This woman, who may not remember her name or where she was born or the name of her children, remembered the most important thing.

LIFE IS LOVE.

I don't think I made it out of that appointment dry eyed. I don't even have a dry eye as I write this now, but I do know that was one of the most powerful lessons I have ever learned. All from listening, all from being present, all from being there.

It is that simple. If you want to unlock the key to living, to not allow another day to pass you by, write that mantra down and stick it everywhere. Set a calendar reminder. Hold it tenderly in your heart. Speak it softly across your lips. Breathe into it.

LIFE IS LOVE.

What if that lesson is the key to it all? Three little words. My mom has taught me so much, but that lesson opened and expanded me in ways I didn't know possible.

It is all love. The pain, the hurt, the grief, the joy, the beauty, the balance, the soft, the strong, the human, the heart, the falling down, the getting back up is all love. We just don't know how to love that big, but I think we can all learn.

Come back home to yourself, to your heart. All the parts of you are there, but are you willing to be loved, to fall in love with yourself, to activate love, to feel it?

How do you do that? How do you move through life knowing it is all love?

First, slow down. Take a big deep breath. Wrap your arms around yourself, hold yourself in this moment. Be here. Stop running.

What are five things about yourself that you are grateful for?

1.

2.

3.

4.

5.

It can be hard to focus on yourself, but can you sit in the discomfort and name three more?

6.

7.

8.

Healing has to happen if you want more peace, more joy, more happiness. It starts here, with yourself, your heart.

We have to learn how to process grief, pain, resentment. We have to learn how to soften our hearts.

I will always suggest gratitude. For me, it's the path that led me here. It's where I learned how to hold the duality of being alive, the good and bad, the pain and joy, the love and grief. So of course start there.

We also have to remember, it's all learned. We show up with the stories we've been told, not necessarily the ones we know to be true. Are we willing to unlearn those generational patterns and stories?

We show up with our grief and fear. We show up with weaknesses we've tried to squeeze into a tiny box before anyone can see them. We show up tattered and torn. We show up exhausted and anxious. We show up armored. We show up ready for a battle. What if we just showed up?

What if we stopped and looked at the person across from us. What if we saw ourselves in that person? Knowing that they too are showing up with their own baggage, their own stories, their own answers. What if we allowed them to be fully there and, perhaps the most important, we allowed ourselves to be fully there too.

We can meet people exactly where they are and also honor our intuition or what our gut tells us about someone when we slow down and tune in.

My dad and I have this conversation a lot.

I say the common thing we all want is to be seen.
He says the common thing we all want is to be loved.

I agree. I desire to be loved. I think being seen is the path to love.

Life is love. Life is love when we are willing to be our whole selves, sharing how we fall and get back up again.

What the hell does it even mean being our whole selves?

The belief we are enough?
The belief we belong?
The belief that we are worth being seen?

The work starts with acknowledging when you have been told that you aren't enough, that you don't belong, and that you aren't worthy of being seen. We've all been told this at some point in our lives, and I believe we can also put ourselves back together, unlearn those lessons, ignore the words telling you are not enough. Bring compassion into our hearts and see that we are all broken. In our own brokenness we see the beauty of each other.

The pressure of performance. The pressure of perfection. The pressure of social media. The pressure of battling our own worries and disbelief. Are we showing our whole selves or are we showing only the "A" reels?

Do you know about **Kintsugi**, the Japanese art of repairing pottery and filling the cracks with gold? That is what healing looks like. That is the image I see when I look at you, when I look at myself in the mirror, when I show up to a meeting, when I am sad or frustrated. We are all cracked, and we all have the ability to fill the cracks with gold.

Choose living. Choose joy.

What if every day for the next thirty days you wrote Life is Love in your journal? How does that help you stretch more in love and less in worry?

I'm not sure, but I know I am willing. Worry less. Love more.

Are you willing?

For the next thirty days in your journal, or on the pages of this book, write:

Five things you are grateful for.
Write **Life is Love** five times.

Set it on your calendar. Notice if your heart begins to soften. Can you hold your own hand and feel the healing that is happening?

Healing takes action. The small steps woven throughout this book are simple action steps, a beginning and a reminder that it is never too late to begin. Ever.

I am grateful for:

1.

2.

3.

4.

5.

Life is Love
Life is Love
Life is Love
Life is Love
Life is Love

10 Minute Noodle Soup

After my ex-husband moved out I didn't know how to cook nor did I have any desire, but I also knew I needed to eat something. I started making this quick 10 minute noodle soup that was packed with veggies, always felt healing and tasted delicious!

Serves 1

Ingredients:

  1 pack of rice noodles (my favorite brand is MAMA Instant Rice Noodles)
  2 cups broth (I use 1 vegan chik'n bouillon cube)
  2 cups sliced veggies (broccoli, carrot, red onion, mushrooms work well too)
  1 tsp Braggs Aminos (or soy sauce)
  1 tsp fresh grated ginger

Instructions:

Bring broth to low boil, add veggies & cook 3-4 minutes.
Add Braggs & ginger.
Add noodles & cook til done (4-5 minutes)
Top with Chili Crisp if you need a little more spice, like I do!
Put it in a big ass bowl & enjoy!

six

The Work

My mom was a worker. She worked until the day she died. I suppose coming from nothing and always craving something was the driver.

Growing up, no matter what she was doing or into, she always wanted more.

"I wish I did that."

"Oh, I should have done that."

"Well, dammit I could've done that."

My mom is the reason I am an entrepreneur. She is the reason why, when Rosalee was five and a half months old, I jumped in not knowing what the future held or how in the heck I was going to do it, but I knew I had to.

I wish I could ask her now if that was drive or dissatisfaction with her life. I wish I asked her more questions; she may not have given me answers, but it might have brought comfort knowing I tried. Those answers wouldn't have changed a thing, and there's comfort there too.

Instead, as a little girl grew inside my belly, I knew I couldn't do the same thing to her. Oh Rosie, I wish I woulda, shoulda, coulda…

Instead, I knew I had to do it. I had to take action on my wants, dreams, wishes, desires, even if I had no clue what in the hell I was doing.

In April 2010, with a five month old strapped to my back and $1,000 from our tax return, my very first company was started—Grateful Grahams. We made delish artisanal handmade graham crackers. We were a gratitude company that made a cookie, not a cookie company that talked about gratitude.

I believed those words and I didn't want Rosalee to watch me be unhappy in a job or trying to put pieces together. I wanted to get to work and show her that her dreams can come true through vision, hard work, belief in herself, and allowing her purpose to flourish.

Over the years, so many women told me they would start working on their dreams once the kids were old enough. But my kids are here with me during my peak time of creativity, so I make them a part of it. My kids have been woven into everything I build, from babies crawling to steal cookies off the cookie tray to working events to sitting in the audience during the Power to Pursue summit. As hard as it was growing businesses with babies I am absolutely blown away that they are witnessing me consistently pushing towards my goals and dreams!

I started in my home baking twenty four grahams at a time, packaging covering corners of our small dining room, friends coming over to hold a baby or tie ribbons on packages. I remember when we created our first banner for Grateful Grahams, it was a $3 yellow sheet from Walmart. Friends came over, we painted our name on it and asked each person to place a handprint because this dream of mine has always been bigger than me. It's my purpose to bring gratitude into your home and into your heart. I used that banner for two years before I finally invested in a real one.

This is a reminder to start with what you have, where you are at. Get out of your own way.

For the last fifteen years I have been creating. Folks have called me a visionary and it's a title I am trying to grow into each day. All I know is that I have been building my visions. Answered prayers. An unfolding. Each step is as beautiful and surprising as the next.

As Grateful Grahams grew, I needed more space for production but couldn't afford to do that on my own, so I asked myself why I couldn't create a shared kitchen space for other small food companies. My nonprofit, the Incubator Kitchen Collective, came into being to meet a need for me and my community, to support food entrepreneurs through the lens that healthy people build healthy businesses.

The Incubator is the land of the dreams. It's a living, breathing community of strong personalities and big ideas. I witness folks coming in with an idea, thought, dream, recipe and MAKE IT. Then make it over and over; make it better and smarter and bigger. It's WILD stepping back to see that hundreds of people got a chance to try out their dream because I was willing to try too. Statistics say 95% of businesses close within the first year! I think we flip that on its head, 95% of our companies are still going after the first year, which means a lot to me. This vision is working for the whole and that's important.

I created a community of believers, believers of their own selves. Their own self worth. Their own dreams. Their own hard work. I get to witness that every day. Startups taking a leap. Pushing the shoulda/woulda/couldas to the side and stepping into their own greatness. A place where folks show up every day and work together for their beliefs. This is like the little engine that can and does. We've supported over 200 startups here in the Greater Cincinnati region. People are showing up to be supported in creating their vision. I am in awe of this body of work, that I get to watch people living their dreams daily. I get to build an organization that supports them at the beginning, with where they are and what they have, helping get them where they want to go.

Do you know how many times I've been questioned? Told it won't ever work? I don't get it, Rachel. Why?

Once, a woman looked me directly in the eyes and told me, "You do too much, you will die." Oh dearest, yes, I will, and one day you will too. And I know I will have savored every second of this delicious life. I show up every day for this work, this belief that my light can help others.

"How will you ever make money off of gratitude," one of the "mentors" asked me, "I've never seen it done before." I responded gently with, "I am not sure how, but I sure am willing to try."

I think about those two comments often. How quick we are to put our own limitations on another. Is it fear or lack of our own belief or worth?

Friends, you are also going to die. So as poet Mary Oliver puts it, "Tell me, what is it you plan to do with your one wild and precious life?"

What is a dream you hold? Perhaps it's still in the bottle? Perhaps you're letting it bubble out? Permission to let it spill out a little here...

♥

♥

♥

Creating the IKC, I was stretched and grew in so many ways, giving me more confidence in myself. I started craving and praying for more. Gratitude and community at the forefront of whatever was next to come.

What's next? How do I continue growing and dreaming and creating?

Every "thing" I have built has been from a vision, the prayer of sharing the message of gratitude and building community. I didn't set out to open a kitchen, I didn't set out to make a deck of cards for inspiration, I didn't set out to build summits for women. I tell folks often this all started with a square brown cookie and a drive to break that generational woulda/coulda/shoulda pattern. Each project, product, event and company is an answered prayer, and I have learned to embrace that instead of fighting it. Trust me, I have tried a ton of things on this journey and there have been more failures than successes.

Ask, then get out of the way and receive the vision. Allow your desires to surface. For me this is entrepreneurship. The projects push me toward my purpose. They keep inching me closer to my truest self. Each thing I build helps me see clearer: my heart, my ability, my love, my gratitude.

My mom worked for me on and off for years. She was there at the beginning of Grateful Grahams where she helped develop a couple of recipes that we sold at the markets and events.

If you've been around a while then maybe you remember our grahamwiches or really her specialty, the buckeye brownie. She helped at events and it was always a hoot because she would sell out of her items and then try to sell the rest of our inventory. This just made me laugh out loud. She would entice you with her sweet little demeanor and before we knew it, she had a buckeye brownie fan club.

I worked with my mom a lot longer than I realize sometimes. I used to work for a national grocer doing marketing and I brought her on to lead our cooking classes because no matter what, you can't beat a mama's cooking. Even then she did it her way, I remember spending hours getting the cooking classes planned out with her each month & she'd come in that day for our marketed Italian class & tell me - "Rach, I found a recipe for this new dish & we're going to make that tonight". No Mary, people are expecting an Italian class & she'd say, ahh it will be fine and her cooking class fan club always was fine with it, even when it drove me crazy & created more work.

I think working with me on and off gave her a new sense of purpose, and it allowed me to always have someone in my corner. My mom always believed in me, especially the days that I couldn't.

Fast forward to 2020. The day Gratitude Grams gifted me with its vision I was sitting right next to her hospital bed. Watching machines breathe for her, not knowing if we would ever get a proper goodbye or another hello. My prayer that day was, "God, I am here and I am grateful, show me how to get through this. Give me a sign of strength, of love. I need a new tool to help me."

This is how Gratitude Grams was born. For about a week I would work on them in the waiting room with my family, in her room while nurses moved about, at home when I couldn't think or do any more.

52 cards.

All paintings of exploration, of grief, of answered prayers.

Words, mantras, phrases that I have used for more than twenty years, each one came flooding in, waking me up.

A new tool for our toolbox.

Maybe that was one of her last gifts to me, a vision of hope. "This is going to hurt sis but you are going to get through it."

Friends, get quiet here for just a moment.

If you have a deck of cards, grab them, sit here with me.

Take a deep breath. Fill up your belly. Don't push through this.

Be here now.

I prayed for visions and peace and understanding.
I offer this moment to you. What is your prayer? What do you need right now? Bring it to the present. Write it down:

Allow your prayer to be here in this space with us, believe it is real. Don't try to control or worry how, just let it be here. In this safe space between us.

I pulled a card just now, while writing this page, to help navigate these pages, to remind us we are all divine beings worthy of answered prayers.

Our card: **You Were Made to Shine.**

Shine on my friends, shine on.

Any time I think of the light shining brighter, I always come back to that Leonard Cohen song "**Anthem**...there is a crack in everything, that's how the light gets in."

YOU
WERE MADE
TO SHINE

 RACHEL DESROCHERS

Holding space for death

I remember this space, this feeling. That death was imminent as we all sat at his bedside when my grandpa, Greats as the kids called him, passed two years ago. Her day may not be days away, but we all know it's coming. A daily decline. Feeble body. Open heart. One foot in each world.

I've cried every time I've said out loud - my mother is dying. I find myself in a different space right now.

Part mother.
Part daughter.
Part doula.
Part space maker.
Part holder of sacred things.
Part doer.
Part mourner.
All gratitude.
Holding space for my mother.

This space is actionable—helping take care of her home, of her, of my dad. This space just welcomed in a new stillness we've yet to feel. This space is sacred, it's holy.

You feel the divine here.

In my mind I picture her surrounded by us, her living angels, but in my heart, I know she's surrounded by her guardian angels, her brothers and sisters who've gone before her—her mom, her dad, Greats and uncle Freddie, too. I know she knows they're there too.

A few weeks ago, after the nurse told us she's in her final stages, she pulled me close and whispered so clearly, "I'm so worried about dying."

All I could do was pull her a little closer and whisper back, "We love you, we're safe, dad's in good hands, and you are ok. You are safe, Mom."

This is death.

I've died. You've died. We've all learned new ways. We've all let someone or something go. How many times do we die before we are no longer afraid of living?

Perhaps that's what this is all about.

Living. My mother is still living, and she will live on in ways I can't see yet.

Today, for her, I ask you to ask yourself - Am I living or dying? Y'all be honest. A lot of us don't know what living is because it lies on the other side of the fear, of the pain, of the anxiety.

Today, please, commit to living. You've been given this one divine and holy life. Create your masterpiece, start the work, say yes, believe, don't stay broken, start living.

And so it is!

Rachel (and all her guardian angels)

My work is a dedication to her.

Reminding her that she was made for greatness. Reminding me that I was made for greatness. Reminding you that you were made for greatness.

She was still alive when Power to Pursue was an idea. I think the experience of her death the year prior to its launch gave me space and confidence to build it. Seeing her die, I was reminded once again we only have this one life. Am I going to step in and grab it, or am I going to just be ok with it passing me by?

I have to say, by far Power to Pursue is the most aligned and holy body of work that I've created. It is the most heart centered thing I have ever built.

The mission is to create a safe space for women to be seen, heard and loved in. We are building rooms for women to have vulnerable conversations, share their truths, and perhaps for the first time in their lives not feel afraid. It's working. We are building with intention, and as I enter into even more growth, I know Mom is right there with me.

Moving into my parents' house saved my life, and I think building Power to Pursue did too. I am rooted deeply in that mission because lo and behold, it was exactly what I needed as my marriage screeched to a halt. I was trying so hard to be a good wife and didn't realize for so long that what I was enduring was not ok. No one else was speaking about these experiences either. Unconsciously, I built the thing I didn't have and truly desired.

Creating this work in my mom's honor was the best way I could say thank you. Thank you Mom for loving me, for doing the best with what you had, for breaking your own generational traumas, and healing as deep as you could.

I was finally learning to accept my own greatness.

I am still afraid of dying.

But I know now I am no longer afraid of living.

Buffalo Tofu Bowls, inspired by Currito

Rosie asks for this a couple of times a month and while I love eating out as much as the next person, we quickly needed to make a home version for us to enjoy too!

Serves 4

  1 block tofu, drained & pressed
  1 cup buffalo sauce
  1/2 tbs garlic powder
  1/2 tsp salt
  1/2 tsp pepper
  1 tbs olive oil
  4 cups cooked rice
  1 cup shredded carrots (girl just buy the shredded carrots)
  1 cup cucumber, diced
  1/3 cup red onion, diced
  1/2 bunch cilantro, chopped

Instructions:

Cut tofu in bite size pieces. Toss your tofu in salt, pepper & garlic powder.

Heat 1 tbs olive oil in a pan, add tofu and sauté for 10-12 minutes until all sides are cooked. I find the best method is to leave it be for 4-5 minutes on a side before tossing around.

Once tofu is cooked on all sides add 1 cup of buffalo sauce. (Oh boy, your eyes may burn a little from that vinegar sizzle.) I stir it all together real good. Turn off your stove and let it sit for a minute while you assemble.

Assemble your bowls:

   1 cup rice
   1/4 cup carrot & cucumber to each bowl
   1/4 of buffalo tofu

Top with red onion & cilantro and enjoy!

(I also love to add a drizzle of tahini to mine, Rosie likes adding a drizzle of ranch to hers.)

seven

The Goodbye

♥ **August 16, 1957 – September 24, 2020** ♥

A life well lived, Mama.
Grateful to be your daughter.
Grateful for washing machine spelling lessons when I
was little.
Grateful I watched you in the kitchen.
Grateful for the years of working at Grateful Grahams.
Grateful to be here for this journey.
Grateful for all the family vacations.
Grateful for you.

And a huge thank you to everyone who's reached out,
checked on us, sent food, prayed, and loved us fiercely.

We are taking the weekend to rest, grieve, be together,
celebrate, and just have an exhale. Details will come for
her celebration of life, memorial, or big ass party.

With full, aching hearts, we thank you all.

On September 24, 2020, at her home on the hill in her yellow sunroom, her favorite room in the house, my mom took her last breath and went on to the land of milk & honey.

It was a surreal day. Our favorite nurse had just clocked out; we were not expecting mom to go that morning. Her nurses guessed she still had a few days. Not a few hours. Not a few moments.

My aunt and uncle stopped by, my siblings were there, and my dad. Me and, bless these kids, they were in the dining room doing school online. It wasn't time, so everyone took an exhale.

Nesha left to work a bit. Chuck went home to shower.

Cindy and Grams took a walk.

Trey was in the kitchen cooking. The kids were in the dining room getting online lessons.

The nurse said come, come now. I think she is close to passing. Her breathing shifted, you could feel the stillness that I think only death brings. Trey kept cooking, the kids kept learning.

Dad and I sat on a small bench a friend gave us. We sat right there. We held her hand and each other. And that final breath was taken. In awe and disbelief, in grief and gratitude my mom died. Right there, in her home, the home I now own.

Trey walked in. Took a breath, and went back to cooking. He is just like her in that he made sure we were fed.

I remember calling the family saying "Get back."

I remember walking in the dining room moments after her last breath and shutting the kids' laptops without a word.

I remember the peace that landed in our laps knowing she was no longer suffering.

After she passed, I have to say we had the most beautiful couple of hours before the funeral home came to pick her up. It seemed like an entire day or, even weeks, could have passed and now that I write it I am sure my dead mom didn't just stay here all day. But I do remember those last moments with her. I am so glad that we were able to keep her here, in her home, her castle on the hill. She deserved to die this way with her things and us nearby. It was the hardest thing I've done and it was the greatest honor to make sure she was where she wanted to be.

We placed sunflowers around her. We brushed her hair one final time, snipping a braided piece to have a lock of her grays. She had the most beautiful color of gray—my hair is coming in gray and I swear every time I spot a new one I smile. Another way to feel her close to me. We gathered in song and prayer and remembrance, with her, for her. I wish all death could feel this peaceful.

I think it is possible to honor the holiness of dying. Again, for me it goes back to living. To allow this life, the trauma and pain, the heart ache, the joy and jubilation, the glory and the grace. All of it.

I remember singing a woman's honoring song and Amazing Grace. I remember each of us speaking praise and holy words about her and her time on this planet. I remember just being there with her one last time.

The day my mom died, a whole new chapter of my life began.

With mom. Without mom.

We broke probably all of the pandemic rules and threw her one hell of a memorial the next month.

I am still grateful for Morella and The Southgate House for letting us host her celebration of life there. And to be honest, I know she was damn happy. She loved it there. We were there earlier that year with her listening to one of her favorite bands. She stood practically at the stage all night, smiling, dancing, this community watching her, us watching her. She loved music, she loved that space. It held us well.

We invited friends to speak. Casey Campbell, a dear friend and local musician, made us weep with song. Mom was celebrated. She was loved. She was remembered.

My best friends and her best friends handled the details. The food. The plant clippings of her favorite plant, a gift to remember her by.

Her nurses came. Her aids came.
Her family came.
Her friends came. Her community came.

I remember sharing this:

I thought I'd have something poignant and profound written for today.

When Grandpa the Great died two and a half years ago, I wrote "Death. It's a beautiful, holy thing. Going back to this space where there are no machines, just us and our heartbeats and our love, that death. A death where the last breath is taken."

And after watching my mom dance between heaven and earth, oh what a holy thing it is.

I had about seventeen drafts of words I wanted to spew— about the goodness of my mama, the spelling lessons and cooking, oh the cooking.

The loving and the living. And well, I couldn't. It's not that time yet.

So instead, I thought I'd share this from Oriah Mountain Dreamer. I found at least eight copies shoved in various Mary piles and even found a copy she had printed and framed. This poem was introduced to her by Janelle, her teacher in Atlanta. When I reread this, I knew that these were the words to share today to remind us of living like she did every single day.

The Invitation

It doesn't interest me what you do for a living. I want to know what you ache for, and if you dare to dream of meeting your heart's longing.

It doesn't interest me how old you are. I want to know if you will risk looking like a fool for love, for your dream, for the adventure of being alive.

It doesn't interest me what planets are squaring your moon. I want to know if you have touched the center of your own sorrow, if you have been opened by life's betrayals or have become shriveled and closed from fear of further pain. I want to know if you can sit with pain, mine or your own, without moving to hide it or fade it or fix it.

I want to know if you can be with joy, mine or your own, if you can dance with wildness and let the ecstasy fill you to the tips of your fingers and toes without cautioning us to be careful, to be realistic, to remember the limitations of being human.

It doesn't interest me if the story you are telling me is true. I want to know if you can disappoint another to be true to yourself; if you can bear the accusation of betrayal and not betray your own soul; if you can be faithless and therefore trustworthy.

I want to know if you can see Beauty, even when it's not pretty, everyday, and if you can source your own life from its presence.

I want to know if you can live with failure, yours and mine, and still stand on the edge of the lake and shout to the silver of the full moon, "Yes!"

It doesn't interest me to know where you live or how much money you have. I want to know if you can get up, after the night of grief and despair, weary and bruised to the bone and do what needs to be done to feed the children.

It doesn't interest me who you know or how you came to be here. I want to know if you will stand in the center of the fire with me and not shrink back.

It doesn't interest me where or what or with whom you have studied. I want to know what sustains you, from the inside, when all else falls away.

I want to know if you can be alone with yourself and if you truly like the company you keep in the empty moments.

Thank you, Oriah!

I could come back to these words over and over and feel her here. This was Mom's purpose: to expand and love. She did just that. She showed me that no matter where you come from or the means you have, everyone deserves to be loved.

For Ellis, Nana's Chicken Noodle Soup

I've been a vegan for a long time. I like it and it works for me. But nothing feels more special than making my boys a big pot of mom's chicken noodle soup. I watched my mom make this so much growing up and still get happy when I make a batch each year.

Ingredients:

   1 whole chicken
   2 medium yellow onions; 1 diced + 1 cut in half
   6 medium carrots; 4 sliced + 2 cut in large chunks
   5 stalks of celery; 3 diced + 2 cut in large chunks
   1 quart of chicken broth
   1 bag of egg noodles
   Salt and pepper

Instructions:

Add your chicken to a pot along with your larger cut carrot, celery and your onion halves. Cover with water. Add 2 big pinches of salt. Ahh, add one more.

Bring to a boil and turn down to a simmer. Cook for about 2 hours on low, so long that your bird is falling apart and meat is coming right off the bones.

Strain - OVER A BOWL. Do not lose that precious and homemade broth you just created. Place chicken on a plate to cool, discard cooked veggies.

Clean your bird. That's right, get in there and get that meat off. I throw the skin & all bones away and save meat for just a bit.

Rinse your pot & add 1 tbs olive oil.

Add diced onion, salt and cook til translucent.

Add your sliced carrots & diced celery. A pinch of salt & stir. Cook for 5 minutes.

I add my homemade stock to the pot.

Bring to a boil

Now taste it. Well, don't burn your mouth.

Add chicken stock or bouillon to enrich the flavor of your broth.

Add your chicken back to the pot.

While your broth is boiling add your noodles & cook until al dente, about two minutes. Ladle & enjoy.

eight

The Light

I don't consider myself an "expert." That is a word I've just never resonated with. But when I think of gratitude maybe, just maybe, I could be an expert.

I've been practicing gratitude for over three decades. Remember that moment in grade school and my dad teaching me the importance of loving myself? That planted something in me. It changed my entire life and the purpose—there is always light. There is always something to be grateful for.

What has been planted in you? Can you sit still enough to hear it?

I don't think at that moment I knew it was going to be my purpose. No, that happened another decade or so later.

My purpose on this planet is to spread the message of gratitude and build community.

Gratitude has expanded my life in ways there could never be words for. It has carried me through sickness and health, overdrawn bank accounts, emergency surgery, births, deaths, heartache, reconciliation, betrayal, divorce, entrepreneurship, parenting, mentoring, creating and dreaming. It's a constant in every aspect of my life. A simple practice and reminder to come back home to myself. Gratitude meets me on the road for more while reminding me of the enoughness of this very breath.

I know I would not be in business for myself fifteen years later if I didn't have this practice. I feel it in my bones. It has always been a safe landing spot for me.

I want it to be a safe landing spot for you, too.

Don't question its simplicity any longer, just practice. What are you grateful for?

1.

2.

3.

4.

5.

6.

7.

8.

9.

10.

It's been a little over four years since my mom died. The unfolding that has happened since then could possibly be an entire other book even though I've tried to carefully weave it in here. This is me, all of me.

I survived all my firsts.

My first thanksgiving (her favorite), my first Christmas, my first birthday, her birthday, my parents' anniversary, the anniversary of her passing. My first separated holidays, vacations, sick kids.

Some days grief swallowed me so whole I couldn't breathe, perhaps a bit like Jonah and the Whale, that big gulp into darkness, wet and blubbery again. There have been days where I couldn't move or get out of bed, though thankfully those are very far and few between. There are days when I can smell her. There are days that if I could just call one more time, I know all would be right in the world. So many times I wanted to pick up the phone and be comforted the way only a mother knows how to do. There are days that a song comes on and I am transported to the last time I sang it with her ("Dublin Blues" by Guy Clark will forever be sung at the top of my lungs just like we used to do after one too many glasses of wine). There are days, dare I even say weeks, where I don't have a thought of her. And that's ok because I know she is right there any time I need her.

I have developed a passion that whenever I see someone out with their mother, I will usually hug the mother first, whether I've met her before or not. Ninety nine percent of the time, I have to fight back tears.

My mother wasn't perfect but she was the perfect mother for me.

At first, after she passed, I tried to talk to her or force myself to find "signs" that she was there, but then I realized that she is still close, just different than I expected. There are no more hugs, but the love and encouragement are still present and I feel a new calmness. She is now a guardian angel who watches over me, watches over this home and these children I am raising.

What an honor to have such an angel.

On New Years Eve entering into 2024, I wrote these words, reminding myself I can always call her back to the kitchen, the place I will always feel the most connected to her.

> *There have been so many traditions I've let fade away since my mama passed I think that's ordinary*
> *Finding my own footing, my own mothering*
> *Focusing on feeling vs doing, being vs trying*
> *And here I am in my kitchen*
> *Emptying dried beans into one of her old bowls*
> *Fingers dive into the layers, looking for bad ones or the rocks she'd have me search for I've run my fingers through bowls of beans more times than I can count on my fingers and toes*
> *These are the traditions I try to pass on, snapping green beans or picking dried beans*
> *And, for just a moment, her & I are cooking again, a tradition I hope will never fade away, I can always call her back home in the kitchen*
> *For a moment alone with her, before Ellis walks in & I share about the many times I ran my hands through these beans and he peaks in the bowl & I watch the sacredness of this tradition*
> *Black eyed peas on New Year's Day*

I am still working on living - gentle and whole.

Grief showed up at my door and man did I answer. I didn't ignore it. I allowed myself to sit with it and process it. Nothing besides gratitude has taught me more. It's the holiest work, the closest to God and myself I've ever been. It stripped every ounce of my being and taught me how to gently fill it back up with light and love.

When I say light -

I want to walk lighter. I want to laugh more. I want to find joy in the hidden corners. I want my heart to feel whole and healthy. I want these cracks, these life experiences not to be put together with black sticky tar but with that golden paint. Remember the **Kintsugi**? I want to shed old shells to make space for more growth. I want to remember the power of the breath, of being in my body, feeling safe, light, joyfilled, hopeful, grateful, willing, able.

When I say love-

I want it to be the first word out of my mouth when I wake up. I am alive, another day to be here. It's how I want people to remember me. "I felt loved when I met Rachel." It's dripping from my hugs and into my kids' and community's arms. It's feeling seen and accepted for who you truly are.

There is no lack when love is present. Love is seeing another, embracing all of me, gentle with my heart, capable, full, miraculous in its simplicity, hope-filled.

This isn't about not experiencing trauma or hardship or pain. It's about suffering less. I want you to suffer less. I want you to welcome grace to your table. I want you to feel the pain, remember you are safe, and that you are going to get through this.

Here it is again, what is Grace to me. Grace is a soft landing spot, it's doing what my best is on the hardest days, it's being tender with my own self when I push so hard, it's the breath that gives me hope. Grace almost feels like the feather falling, slow & gentle. Offering myself grace, Stephanie my soul sister said "are you being as kind to yourself as you are to your best friend?" That's grace.

When was the last time you offered yourself grace? When you stopped and looked at the load you were carrying? The impact you are making? The work you are doing in your home or office? The way you handled it? The way you loved yourself through it? The way you got back up?

That GRACE.

Today I will offer myself grace by

♥

♥

♥

May we all be more grace-filled. To our own hearts and to each other. It's gratitude in action. It's looking back and saying, "This happened."

I am here. I have a home. I have a car. I have a family. I have dinner on the table. It's not either/or. It's and.

So yes, I want more love and light because they're the supporters of the and.

I fell down AND I got back up.

I lost my mother AND I have memory after memory with her.

I yelled at my kids AND I reminded them how much I love them AND showed them my human "I am sorry" side.

I lost the bid on a project AND sometimes the universe helps us stay on track even when it's not what we think we wanted.

Grace and forgiveness and grief and gratitude have helped me learn the holiness of AND.

I can miss my mother AND I can share with my kids what I miss about her.

I can lose someone to a horrific disease AND I can look back at the videos and pictures of the hilarious phase of Alzheimer's. I will forever be grateful for the times when we laughed and she laughed. We still giggle remembering how she put her shirts on backwards and more than once wore a shirt for her pants.

I will forever remember the weird juxtaposition, the "and" of remembering the fun we had with the shirt for a pair of pants AND the look on her face full of sorrow and surprise when I told her it was my birthday. The image of sorrow on her face will forever burn in my memory. The heartache of not remembering her own child's birth and not knowing it was her birthday.

We can transform the grief with gratitude. That Practice. Do the work, as I like to say. Hold the light and the dark.

Hold the pain and jubilation.

Hold the holy and the unjust. Hold the love and sorrow. Hold the glory and trauma.

We are whole. These experiences make us whole.

Maybe look at your light to dark ratio. Is it all bad? Are you pessimistic about everything that didn't go your way? Are you so unhappy and stuck you can't see beyond that hurt?

Choose to do the practice.

Choose to wake up and name seven things you are grateful for.

Give that practice time. If you wanted to run a marathon you wouldn't just go out and buy brand new shoes and run for twenty miles.

No, you would start with maybe a mile, heck, maybe a half mile or maybe just a walk around the block in those old tennis shoes.

Start today with what you have and where you are. BUT START.

What are you grateful for?

1.

2.

3.

4.

5.

6.

7.

Give it time. Develop the muscle.

Shine light on it every day. Water it, the tending is the important part. When you tend, things start to mend.

I've had this practice for thirty years. I feel honored to share it so deeply here with you on these pages. I'm not so different from you, carrying the weight of the world these last few years. I guess a pandemic will do that to you. A dying mother or divorce will too.

I guess the only constant is change. How many times can our heart shatter and we keep going? How many times are you willing to shed the old shell, like the lobster, to have more room for growth, joy, peace? If I recapped my life since 2018 it would consist of this:

Emergency surgery

100 pounds of weight loss

Gaining custody of a family member for a year

Kid graduating high school & moving out

An investor who defrauded and stole from me and tried to destroy everything I have worked so hard to build

Moving my family into my parents' home (which I eventually bought) to help during her last few months

Losing my mother

Leaving an abusive marriage

Becoming a single parent, again

Kid graduating college. Ya that one, the one I had at eighteen. The one I left college to raise. Man, I am weeping just now saying that out loud. I am proud of him. AND Rebuilding. Getting back up. Every. Single. Time. slowly slowly getting back up.

Healing can't be rushed.

A whirlwind of grief, each time expanding me a bit more. Each time filling my cracks with more gold.

I should have bought stock in Kleenex.

I look at my work too during all of this. I think it just keeps getting better.

With each new grief, I work to be more transparent and vulnerable with my words. The more I share transparently, the more hope I experience. More hope brings more grace. The grace makes space for more gratitude. More gratitude sheds more light. With more light, well you can see where this is going. It's like Rachel's version of "If you give the mouse a cookie" … If you give Rachel a grief sandwich.

Gratitude has saved my life time and time again.

Gratitude brings me hope and grace every single time. It lightens the load.

When I first started writing this book it was for my mother, for her memory. So much has happened since her passing and I now accept that this book has always been for me. Capturing this journey I've been on, how death, divorce and coming back home to myself mattered. The pain and suffering mattered. These words mattered. I matter.

Now I am happy. And being this happy again feels good. I thought I was happy before, but not like this, deep in my bones. Perhaps it was the happiness of surviving and now I am experiencing the happiness of thriving.

I see now that I took all of my pain, the sorrow, the grief and did my damndest to transform it so something good could grow as a result. A purpose. My work.

As I look back at Power to Pursue, I wish my mom was here to witness the magnitude and impact we are having; the women we are supporting and the community we are building. I know she "knows" but I do wish I could look out in the audience and see her smiling. And I know she is there every step of the way with me. Keeping me going on my hardest days. She is reflected now in those mothers, aunts, and sisters who fill our audience. I see her in a new way now.

Power to Pursue reflects my deepest and most vulnerable beliefs. Creating a safe space for women to be seen, heard, and loved. I think in hindsight, that mission unfolded because in my home life it was the thing I was craving the most. Well, if I couldn't have it, I could at least build it for others. Phew. And I feel safe there. I feel seen there. I feel heard there. I feel loved there. More than I ever thought possible. I want every human to experience that, but I want women to know they are worthy of that. They deserve that. That we deserve that. To be loved well. All of us, our quirks and qualms, our good days and our bad days. We are enough.

In these rooms, vulnerability can rise to the surface, topics are no longer taboo, women share how they fall AND get back up. We're talking about everything from personal finance to menopause, sexual well being, how to ask for a raise. We're normalizing talking about what we are all questioning or struggling with. I had to die a thousand deaths to learn that. If I can help anyone suffer less, to have one less death because of my words, my work, my heart then these words will have been worth it.

Vulnerability is one of my superpowers. I love bringing hard topics to the surface. I know that I share deeply and I want to normalize this in place of small talk. So sharing for me, being vulnerable with these words. I need to get them out. Energetically if I didn't I think I would combust. I would explode with pain and suffering. The weight of 1,000 deaths would be in my every breath. Vulnerability has given me freedom.

It's an honor unlike any other.

Permission to grieve and feel and break and heal.

My life's greatest work is healing my heart. To my kids, if you are reading this, you are my life's greatest work, and my healing has allowed me to mother, to be present, to love you deeper because I learned how to love myself deeper.

What if it is all divine? What if it has been divinely orchestrated?

Why death? Why suffering? Why grief?

Maybe for the light. And gold paint. And healing. Rising back to the surface.

I don't know those answers. But I know every "bad" thing has helped me witness more miracles. Every "bad" thing has opened my heart bigger than I ever thought imaginable. Every "bad" thing has filled me back up with purpose and passion. I didn't want my mother to die at sixty-three or have all my money stolen or to dissolve a marriage after being together for twenty years. But without those experiences, maybe these words wouldn't be here or the work wouldn't be so impactful or I wouldn't marvel at the magic of the breath. And so for me, I am grateful.

I am grateful that I listened to her and was at the doctor's office the day she declared LIFE IS LOVE.

I am grateful that I got to pick rocks out of bowls of dried beans.

I am grateful that our fraud case showed me truths about myself that I was unwilling to hear. I am grateful that the fraud case showed me that I am strong and resilient in a way I didn't know before.

I am grateful that I stood up and stopped this man, used my voice and filed charges.

I am grateful I married my ex-husband.
I am grateful for what being sucked bone dry taught me.
I am grateful for what I thought love was because it helped me learn what love really is.

I am grateful I had Camden at eighteen.

I am grateful I started my first company at twenty-four.

I am grateful that I almost lost our house because I was pouring everything into work and had to learn to ask for help, slow down, learn a new way to work.

I am grateful for my children, for what we've learned together and how coming together even stronger post divorce has given us more joy, understanding and freedom.

I am grateful that vulnerability is a superpower of mine.

I am grateful for every single time I have fallen down.

I am grateful for every single time I have gotten back up.

I am grateful for my sisters who have carried me through and nursed me back to health time and time again.

I am grateful for my brother and sister and how our mother's death destroyed each of us differently.

I am grateful for my dad who, every time I have asked for help, has shown up wholeheartedly to listen, support, and guide.

I am grateful for me, my body and my heart and my willingness. People often ask about regrets. Do you regret anything?

I don't. I am not sure there is one thing I would change. Ok ok, maybe the year I almost lost the house - that sucked. Even with valuable lessons, that sucked. But man, not having anything, not having a pot to piss in as they say, that teaches you something.

I don't have any regrets.

Each thing. Each choice. Each call and answer.

It got me here.

Here I am feeling whole.

Here I am embodying all of me.

Here I believe I am worthy. Here I feel like I am enough.

Because of those experiences, those things, those choices.

Maybe it's the learning from the choices that is the key. You choose your own suffering. I didn't choose the time of my mother's death but I did choose how I would best show up for her and for me. I did choose to acknowledge that she did her best; not my best, but her best. And that is holy work.

Gratitude has helped me suffer less. Gratitude has helped me reflect on my choices. Gratitude has helped me know that no matter what, I am here. I can breathe and take up space. I can start again. I can feel pain and joy in a single second. I can do hard things. I can heal. I can work from my heart. I can suffer and heal.

No matter what, I can come back to the practice of gratitude. It can fill my lungs with hope. I can see the glimmers of light through the darkness. I can remember it will be ok. I can realize that it's the tiny things that make the biggest difference.

I have shoes and a coat on cold days. I have a lot of food in my pantry that will feed us. I have people who love me and believe in me. I have work I believe in. I have safe drinking water. I have fingers and a computer I can write at. I have eyes that can see sunrises and sunsets. I have ears that can hear my children laughing or crying. I have a community that supports my work. I have courage to take up space. I have a dad who is still alive. Moving into her home, to tend and mother her, to be here when she took her last breath. It was a miracle in hindsight.

Our marriage was easier on me those last years when we moved into my parents' house, with my mom dying downstairs, with my dad asleep two doors down. Being an entrepreneur saved my life. While I came to realize our marriage was abusive toward me, I was constantly seeking the light. Thanks to gratitude, I always knew it was there, I just had to deepen my practice. It took me twenty years to understand what our marriage was doing to me and that our marriage needed to end.

I worked. I worked harder. I worked the hardest I have ever worked. The little bit I had in reserves I poured it into my visions, into my work and into my kids.

I see that now.

Gratitude saved me. No matter how bad it got, what he did to me, my gratitude practice helped me focus: my kids were safe. I was able to work. I knew my life was worth more. I never stopped practicing no matter how depleted my soul was.

Thank you, Mom. In your death I was saved.

On April 10th 2023 my entire life changed. Every wall around me came crumbling down. The truth was told and in that instant my life shifted in a completely different direction.

Everything stopped. It is as though time stood still. Four weeks before Power to Pursue, the largest event of my life, the largest grief bomb exploded ruthlessly in my lap. I hate that it happened that way, I love that it happened that way. Both of these are truths for me. All at once felt easier than spread out. It was divine timing. I blocked time to recover after the event, to allow myself to process what I had known for 20 years.

Talk about being at max capacity – we had two kids at home and my work was our sole income. I pulled that event off. It was the first event he hadn't been present for, and I still marvel at how I felt when it was over.

I wasn't exhausted. I had an energy that felt new. I didn't share much but I did share that I made it there that morning and I was proud that we all made it there that morning. The world still kept going while I was falling apart. But for the first time in a long time I left that event:

Feeling safe. Feeling grounded. Feeling embodied.

He moved out less than 2 months later. The entire house exhaled. Pain walked out, grace walked in.

I finally started to heal. I finally had memories and dreams coming back to me. That's a bit like purgatory. Seeing how numb you've been, how much in survival mode you've been in.

I didn't cook. I didn't paint. I didn't host. I didn't write for that next year.

Replenishing. Finding myself again. Moving trauma out of my body.

Learning to come home to myself. Learning to feel safe again.

I wrote this on December 12, 2023:

> It's been a long few days for me. A wave of grief washed upon shore. December. Divorce. End of the year, closure. Humaning. Holidays. Kids growing up. Being here in it, with it, trying to find my way to the surface. The duality. The yin and yang - light and dark - suffering and surrender.
>
> It's all brutiful. A friend yesterday reminded me what a gift it is when I go through this, he said - you transmute it and give it back to the rest of us, to help, make it better, see the light, come back to the surface.
>
> An honor, my offering. The light the grief brings.
>
> So, all of this and none of this to say - I am grateful for the grief, the waves, and always, always coming back to the surface. I am incredibly grateful to those of you who jump right in with me and help me get back to shore, no questions asked. I am ok, truly, it's important to show this whole me here. I am proud to be able to share, we're all carrying a load. I hope you feel the light shine on you a bit brighter today - you are worth every moment of shine.
>
> I don't want to bypass the humanity of building, creating, breathing, amen.

Thank you, Mom, for saving me.

I woke up. I recognized and called the trauma what it was. I decided living is ahead of me. I don't have to suffer that way any longer or ever again. I worked with healers, energy workers, light workers, therapists, marma therapy, and astrologists. They all said the same things: you will be better; you will transmute this into the brightest light; you are safe and you are loved. And they are right!

Rachel Smith held me as I processed pieces buried so deep, panicked breath, tears coming harder than I had ever felt, grabbing her hand and holding on. Walking through it. Getting him out of my body.

I've never been afraid of the work whether I was eleven or seventeen or forty.

Thank you, Mom, for dying. So that I could find myself, my voice, my body, my heart again. And for that I am grateful.

Hold the hurt lightly. Hold your heart bravely.

That is what these pages have been for me.

Sharing the mess. The look behind the curtains. The girl who worked harder and prayed harder. The girl who knew the purpose was greater than the pain. Who didn't know the terms for what she endured until it was too late and also knowing it was never too late.

And I am still standing. I am here and more willing to live than I have ever been before.

I am **kintsugi**-ing the shit out of myself. Gold peeking out of every crack. I know now how to suffer less. I am still not afraid of suffering. I am safe.

Healing takes time. This is life work, not today work. I say that often when meeting other people and sharing my story. Slow down. Notice the dew on the grass. Notice the pain in your heart. Notice the sun shining through. Don't be afraid to be broken, but maybe more importantly, don't be afraid to put yourself back together.

I told a girlfriend, "It's the putting us back together, those cracked pieces, that's us. Painted in gold. As whole as brokenness can be."

As whole as we can be when death is at our doorstep.

Grief is hard. These words are pouring out of me, I want to normalize that. But in my experience ignoring the grief, pushing down the grief, not acknowledging the grief, that is harder.

I hope these words help you be less afraid of grief. To look it in the eyes. To find the light against so much darkness.

I encourage you to start.

Start looking and allowing. Start with gratitude.

Again - here is a page for that practice.

Can you name twelve things to be grateful for?

1.

2.

3.

4.

5.

6.

7.

8.

9.

10.

11.

12.

In all of these pages, in all of this practice, a question...

Have you named yourself yet?

Have you allowed YOU to show up here? I hope so. If not...Are you willing?

I love you. Thank you for being here on these pages with me. For believing in me.

I am grateful for you. I am grateful for these experiences. I am grateful to be here, alive with more hope and a deeper belief in love than I ever thought possible. What a gift.

Chocolate Chip Pancakes

Now, this even feels silly putting this in here but when I asked my kids what I cook a lot & food they actually EAT everyone agreed - mom you make really good pancakes. Well, thank you very much Bisquick, I mean kids.

So it's Sunday morning and you want to give your kids a little treat?

Ingredients:

3 cups Bisquick
3 eggs (I will sneak the extra stuff in anywhere I can)
2 cups whole milk (or milk of your choice)
1 tbs oil (I typically use olive or vegetable oil)
1 cup mini chocolate chips
Butter
Strawberries, sliced
Pure maple syrup
Whipped cream (ya know, if they've been extra good and put their laundry away)

Instructions:

Mix Bisquick, eggs, milk & 1 tbs oil together.
Get your skillet medium heat. Add about 1 tbs butter to pan. Let it melt and get all over. Ladle or scoop your batter to the pan, and then sprinkle chocolate chips into each pancake. Carefully flip your pancakes, cooking thoroughly.
 Keep 'em going until you've cooked all of your batter.

Lay out your pancakes, sliced strawberries, whipped cream, and maple syrup and let the Family Brunch begin. Ellis will crush 5+ pancakes.

about the author

Rachel DesRochers is an inspiring entrepreneur, author, and community leader dedicated to spreading gratitude and fostering connections through her work. She is the founder of The Gratitude Collective, a platform built on the principles of kindness, mindfulness, and appreciation, which serves as the foundation for her various ventures.

As an author, Rachel shares her transformative journey through **The Mourning Light**, a heartfelt exploration of healing, resilience, and growth. Paired with the accompanying journal, **Shift to Light - 90 Days to Grateful**, Rachel provides practical tools for cultivating gratitude and embracing personal transformation.

Rachel resides in Cincinnati, Ohio, with her three wonderful children, Camden, Rosie, and Ellis. Her family inspires her to live with gratitude and purpose, and their support fuels her passion for creating meaningful connections and purpose-driven work.

about the artist team

The team at **fenbury** designed **Shift to Light: 90 Days to Gratitude**, the companion to this book, and the artwork here in **The Mourning Light**.

fenbury is an agency on a mission to build meaningful brands, fueled by our passion and purpose. We are a women-owned and women-led firm that is transforming the world around us.

We partner with extraordinary clients, and together make the world a better place. There is nothing more rewarding than helping our clients' brands grow and evolve—and watching them succeed.

We build things that matter.

We meet you where you are and elevate your brand to the next level.

fenbury.com

about VITALITY

VITALITY is a circle of friends welcoming all, awakening each other, and reminding each other that we are Whole. Our affordable self-care programs invite everyone to move, to breathe, to rest, to contemplate, to grow... wherever each person begins their self-care journey, wherever and however they want to become.

It's the power of a circle!

We invite you to explore with us through our

donation-based classes...in person & via Zoom
affordable trainings
individual sessions
volunteer opportunities

vitalitycincinnati.org

VITALITY

buzz, bliss + books

publishing books from VITALITY's circle of friends
inspiring love, creativity, + possibility

vitalitybuzz.org

www.ingramcontent.com/pod-product-compliance
Lightning Source LLC
Chambersburg PA
CBHW061808120626
46550CB00005B/2186